Counselling

ETHEL VENABLES
University of Aston in Birmingham

LONDON
The National Marriage Guidance Council
1971

This book first published 1971 *by*
NATIONAL MARRIAGE GUIDANCE COUNCIL
58 Queen Anne Street, London W1M 0BT

Printed in Great Britain by
Bradleys, Reading and London

SBN 85351 008 3 (paperback)

SBN 85351 009 1 (hardback)

Contents

Preface

Like teaching, counselling is an art. There are no easy right answers which can be looked up in a book of reference for the problems which clients bring to counsellors. People in trouble usually have a few kind and sympathetic friends or neighbours and although the counsellor must be a warm and friendly person too, he must clearly be able to offer something more. This book provides some answers to the question:—'What have counsellors to offer, that friendly relatives, neighbours and youth workers are not usually able to provide?'

Parents sometimes wonder whether it would benefit their children if they were to read a psychology textbook. There can be no 'yes–no' answer to this question, nor is there for counsellors who have a similar problem. The answer 'yes' is dangerous because theory without feeling and involvement is useless: 'no' is hard on the psychologists since it implies that they are wasting their time. The only answer is that it depends on the effect of the book upon the reader. At first, no doubt, it can get in the way of any effective relationship. The mother who stops to consult Dr Spock before giving her child a hug when he is crying is not, in fact, following Dr Spock; to do this she needs to assimilate his views and make them her own. Similarly for counsellors, one of whom once said to me, 'Before I read Carl Rogers I was jolly good—helped all sorts of people—now I'm useless'.

The *assimilation* of new knowledge, as distinct from rote learning of rules, is a slow and largely unconscious process which is encouraged when book learning and theorising are combined with practice. For the successful practice of an art there must be a continuing willingness to learn. Each child, each client, being unique can teach us something new, thus training for counselling cannot be considered a once for all affair. It must be a continuing on-the-job commitment.

In discussing psychological theories related to counselling there is no suggestion that people can only be helped by those who possess such knowledge. What is implied is that if those who practise counselling and those who teach it want to remain alert to their own shortcomings and to go on increasing their effectiveness, some such framework within which to examine their work is essential.

As the theorists make abundantly clear any attempt to discuss human interaction in a face to face situation, without involving oneself as a person is bound to fail; the same is probably true when one is writing about it. So I make no apology for the use of personal examples in this book.

However, I do not think that these necessarily make much impact on the reader. The kind of learning that takes place in case discussion or in the counselling room is largely if not entirely incommunicable. Typescripts of interviews and discussions, deprived as they are of the feelings that have been aroused, usually seem to me to be trite and rather dull. The 'Aha' reaction to a sudden insight is an individual experience and trying to convey the feeling in words is probably doomed to failure. Nevertheless the attempt must be made not only for the sake of would-be students but also in order to give some answer to the general public who quite properly wish to know what this word 'counselling' means.

Professionally I am an Educational Psychologist and I have worked with young people not only as a counsellor but as a teacher in a school and occasionally in a youth club, and as a lecturer in technical colleges and universities. My main job has been as a research worker among technical college students. My interest in the learning process and in theories about human development was of course stimulated and informed by my academic studies, but I owe my interest in counselling and in psychodynamics to the National Marriage Guidance Council. I was accepted for training as a counsellor in 1950 and am much indebted to the three men who were in charge of training and assessment for the NMGC at that time: Alan Ingleby, Reg

Pestell[1] and John Wallis. I worked with them all for many years; each taught me a great deal and I am pleased to have this opportunity to pay a tribute to their work. They cannot be held responsible for the content of the book but it was they who in various ways stimulated me to explore the theoretical basis of counselling practice and to try to expound it.

I am grateful to several colleagues for answering my questions and helping me to clarify my thoughts but want to thank in particular Mrs Angela Reed for her understanding help and wise comments, her patience over deadlines which were never kept and her expertise in transforming a typescript into a printed page.

ETHEL VENABLES

December, 1970

1. Now The Rt. Hon. The Lord Wells-Pestell of Combs.

Chapter 1

The Place of the Counsellor in the Pattern of Social Work

The word 'Counsel' has returned to these shores, a little debased perhaps by its commercial connections. Florists and the makers of spectacle frames now offer to 'counsel' us on the appropriate use of their products, but here we are discussing its use in relation to more serious dilemmas.

It is an old and biblical word which came to be mainly restricted to the legal profession. It travelled to the New World, presumably on the *Mayflower*, and we owe its recent revival to the Americans.

It springs from the same root as consul, consult, conciliate: it suggests deliberation, a two-way process, an interchange. There is an expectation that it will be wise—that there will be no snap judgements. One dictionary defines counsel as 'secret purpose, or the secrets entrusted in consultation'.

'Take no counsel of a fool' advises Chaucer, and Job in his agony cries, 'Who is this that darkeneth counsel with words without knowledge'. God, he says, 'hath Counsel and understanding'.

WHY NOW?

The process then is as old as the hills and people in crises of indecision have always sought out those with a reputation for wisdom to help them solve their problems. So why in the middle of the twentieth century is there such an upsurge of interest, such a widespread recognition of a need to offer help of this kind to—the married and the divorced; to widows and widowers; engaged couples, students, young people at school or in youth clubs, their parents, the elderly, the lonely, indeed—any man, woman or child with a personal problem.

The great concern with human problems at this point in time is no accident. Man's struggle to conquer his environment and to solve the scientific and technological problems is won. We now even have the time, energy and resources to attempt to conquer outer space. In saying this I am not callously forgetting the poverty that still exists, nor the struggles of the emerging countries to catch up with the twentieth century. The point is that we *can* conquer these material problems—we have the scientific and technical know-how to do so. Catching up will take time, but it will happen. From now on the major focus of struggle is not with external nature, but with our own internal human nature.

Everywhere we look there are problems of human relationships; between parents and children, men and women, teachers and pupils, managers and workers, dons and students; between races and between nations; between the governors and the governed. We have had something like a thousand years of advance in the physical sciences and fifty or sixty years trying to arrive at some scientific understanding of people. Peter Medawar chose as the title of a book of essays 'The Art of the Soluble'.[1] Scientists, he argues, are practical men and their business is to solve problems. They tackle the most important of the problems which they think they *can* solve: thus the simpler problems are solved first. Certainly the constructing of a computer is simpler than understanding the working of the human brain.

While we fight for bread, personal relationships are unlikely to be of a very subtle kind. Authoritarian regimes precede the democratic ones and not *vice versa.* When a man was the autocratic head of his family and his wife and children chattels, there were fewer divorces; but no one should make the mistake of thinking that this is a sign that the quality of married life has deteriorated. The change from boss to partner is difficult but more exciting and there is no going back; the order of events is inexorable. The more civilised we become, the more our animal needs are catered for, the more we are made aware of our *human* nature and its particular needs. The future of civilisation now depends upon our capacity to deal with ourselves.

Scientific method in relation to the physical sciences is associated in our minds with weighing and measuring but we all know that we cannot get very far in understanding our children simply by weighing and measuring them and ensuring that they are properly clad. Indeed to concern ourselves solely with their physical well-being would be totally *un*scientific. Measurement is meaningless unless applied to the appropriate data and the most important data about people are not their vital statistics but those relating to their hopes and fears, loves and hates, satisfactions and frustrations and to companionship and loneliness. These, together with the mastery of a language in which to discuss them, are the essentially human attributes which distinguish us from the rest of the animal kingdom.

The social scientist is not then dealing with static inanimate objects but with dynamic human subjects who potentially, at least, have the power to frustrate his investigations and give the lie to his findings. They can—and do—resist his examinations. That there is a resistance to discussing one's mental condition is hardly surprising. In the early days of medicine, people were often afraid to have their bodies examined and humane sympathetic treatment of mental breakdown is relatively recent. Preventive medicine and the positive promotion of bodily health is now well accepted; the promotion of mental health, involving the recognition of signs of stress and attempts to resolve anxieties is new.

IS COUNSELLING JUST ANOTHER NAME FOR ADVISING?

There is much confusion about the nature of the counselling process and judging by the growing popularity of the term, counselling would seem to be regarded as an activity superior to that of an adviser. Sometimes the words are interchanged, suggesting that it is somehow better—even morally superior—to 'counsel' people rather than to offer them advice. This is nonsense. Advice is the prerogative of the experts: they *know*—what to do with broken arms, where different kinds of schools and colleges are to be found, how to set about finding a job, or getting a divorce. If, however, Mr Smith falls out with his wife or Master Smith rejects his father, where is the expert who can tell them how to improve their relationships? We may urge them to forget their hatred and love each other better, but if they could do that they would have no problem and no need of our help. They 'know' they 'shouldn't' do these things—they have undoubtedly been told so many times. Their problem is not that they 'won't' put things right, but that they 'can't'. Mr Jones' solution might be a bunch of flowers because that's the way he manages to convince Mrs Jones that he loves her; but if buying flowers is out of character for Mr Smith, then his wife's suspicions might well be increased. If he feels so guilty, there must be something to hide! To suggest cheerful ready-made solutions is insensitive and may well do more harm than good. Counsellors who are trying to help people with emotional problems don't despise advice; they give it themselves—of an appropriate kind. By their very existence they are 'saying' to people—'when you are in trouble with emotional tangles and relationship problems, we advise you to take time to come and talk about them. In our experience this can be of enormous help.' Straightforward advice from the expert—in counselling. However when the dialogue begins, what the Smith family needs is an impartial ear, not an adviser. Counsellors cannot advise them—this is not an 'If I were you . . . ' situation. The only potential experts are the Smiths and they need help to explore their position and to see the problem through the eyes of the other members of the family. The counsellor can feed back to them what they seem to be saying and help them to express their antagonisms and hurt feelings and so to grope towards a discovery of how best to tackle the issues. Trying to promote happy endings before the people concerned have taken time to discover the basic problems which underlie their day to day difficulties is useless. There may *indeed* be another woman and Smith junior may decide he *must* leave home: the ending may not be an immediately happy one, but if the true situation is faced the future is likely to be emotionally healthier.

The view of man implicit in this approach to his personal difficulties which we owe to Freud has become part of the social climate of our day. Following the initial storm of controversy provoked by Freud's writings a calmer climate now prevails in which rational discussion and scientific investigation are possible.

Nevertheless it has to be recognised that the patience and devotion of psychiatrists and other psychotherapists, social workers and counsellors is motivated as much by a particular philosophic stance and a faith in progress—a faith that man is 'helpable'—as by any scientific evidence. Paul Halmos in his book 'The Faith of the Counsellors'[2] examines this point in detail. He considers that 'the practitioners' of what he calls this 'caring—listening—prompting' expertise are 'a new social factor of considerable influence on the cultural and moral changes in twentieth century western society'.[3]

We shall return to this question in Chapter 2, but first we need to separate his 'counsellors' into their various categories and attempt to differentiate their various roles.

What then is the difference between psychotherapy, social case work and counselling? There is no agreement about this and any attempt at clarification must, at this stage, be a personal one. The following simple analysis is presented not as dogma but as a working hypothesis.

In the first place the counsellor has one job; the others—therapists and social workers—several. Psychiatrists do their specialist training in mental illness after their general training as physicians. Thus they are uniquely equipped to investigate possible physical concomitants of mental symptoms and they are in a key position where the distinctions between physical and mental illness break down. Physical treatments, either electrical or by means of chemicals, for what were traditionally regarded as mental illnesses, underline the fact that the brain is a physical organ and it is no longer possible to make rigid distinctions between the malfunctioning of the cells of the brain and the breakdown of the cells of the liver. Indeed there is a growing body of psychiatrists who regard the physical/mental dichotomy as meaningless and look forward to the demise of the separate mental institution and the enlargement of general hospitals to equip them to deal with all forms of ill health.

There are several areas of mental abnormality in which psychiatrists specialise. Perhaps the most important distinction is that between mental illness and subnormality and mental defect. The latter term includes a great variety of conditions including subnormal intelligence, the specific abnormalities of the mongol, pre- and post-natal brain damage and the severe defect of the helpless imbecile.

In the field of mental *illness* classical psychiatry recognises two types—the neuroses and the psychoses. Treatment of course varies with the symptoms including constraints for the severe psychotic to avoid self-destruction, anti-depressant pills for the mildly neurotic and 'talking cures'. The latter vary from prolonged analysis of dreams and free associations with Freudian psychoanalysts to relatively brief sessions with psychotherapists in out-patients clinics.

Psychotherapy strictly defined means treatment by psychological methods but the term as at present used implies an eclectic approach to the patient free from too close an adherence to any particular technique. As far as method is concerned, the process of counselling is very similar. The major distinction is in the relationship. In the doctor's consulting room or the psychiatric clinic the relationship, though it might be disguised by a friendly and relaxed atmosphere, is nevertheless that of a doctor to his patient: there is an assumption of possible illness. In the counselling room the assumption is quite other. The client is dealt with as a 'normal' person in trouble. If you fall out with your wife, or your husband dies or your children run away from home or you go bankrupt, it is perfectly normal to be distressed. It would be abnormal to take no notice and make no fuss. To need to talk, to pour it all out, is a normal reaction in such a case; if there is no one to turn to who has the time or the willingness to listen, then in the interests of mental health some trained and friendly ear should be available.[4]

The two assumptions—that in the one case the patient is ill and in the other that the client is normal—may not be borne out in practice. Many sick people reach the counsellor's room, not infrequently complaining that a spouse is mad and should be locked up, and the counsellor's job is to persuade them to seek the appropriate help, with the assistance of the unfortunate spouse, wherever possible. As the psychiatrist becomes a much less frightening figure more and more normal people seek his help in the solution of their problems and more and more psychiatrists are looking for lay counsellors to deal with them. The distinction is not by any means cut and dried—the edges are very blurred. Often a psychiatrist will offer a client a diagnostic interview and then give the counsellor moral support while he—the counsellor—continues to try to help. If we are to provide all the help that is needed this two-way traffic must continue to increase. In borderline cases the assumption of normality and the availability of help outside the medical profession probably has positive benefits. We are now much more aware of the harm done to a person's self-esteem by the premature imposition of a damaging label.

The complexities of civilised living provide numerous areas where social breakdown is possible and each area tends to have its own statutory group of social workers. The demarcation is usually explicit in their titles—probation officers, child care workers, prison officers, mental welfare workers, psychiatric social workers and so on, but their training covers a great deal of common ground. Indeed plans for the future such as those outlined in the Seebohm Report[5] envisage a generic training course for all social workers, any specific skills being acquired as and when needed. Such a scheme would make it possible for personnel to move more easily between the various services but the opposing point of view—more and better specialised training—is not without its adherents.

In all the areas mentioned breakdown is associated with some failure in human relationships and for most of these groups of workers this is a major concern. They do, however, have other tasks, often of a more practical nature, and workers frequently complain that because of their heavy case loads they have insufficient time to deal adequately with the emotional problems of their clients.

Not all social work training involves satisfactory training in counselling, but for some, such as psychiatric social workers, this is a main focus, though they use the term 'casework'. The difference in terminology is valuable because there are at least two major differences between the two roles—one concerned with outcomes and the other with relationships. The social workers, however sympathetic to the personal problems of their clients, are, in most instances, involved in decisions of a practical kind; should they recommend that the child be taken into care, that this adolescent would benefit from a period in an approved school, that this mental patient should not continue to live at home and so on.

Relationships also differ, whether the caseworker likes it or not (and he frequently does not). A statutory worker is an authority figure and his counselling has to be done against that background. Not every probation officer agrees with the law or with the penal treatment of adolescent delinquents, nor is the prison officer always happy with the government of prisons. This is also the dilemma of the social worker who feels the need to be a social reformer, and it is a very real one. Counsellors who are employed by a statutory body have similar difficulties as many of the newly trained teacher-counsellors are beginning to discover. Such conflicts are special cases of an overriding dilemma at the heart of all 'helping' services and the counsellor working on his own or for a voluntary body, though he has more protection, cannot entirely escape. The basic question is Who or What are we trying to help? Are we agents for social conformity or social change? What is a 'well-adjusted' person? A rebel adjusted to his own values or a conformer suppressing his own individuality? Or someone doing a balancing act in between these extremes?

THE ROLE OF THE COUNSELLOR

How do we see a counsellor—what sort of person is he?[6] He must first of all have some social skills and be able to establish easy and confident relationships with a client from the outset. He must be able to listen, not only with his ears, but with all his senses, to what this person in distress is conveying to him and he must be able to tolerate the message whatever it is. He must attempt to discriminate between the important issues and the trivial ones, checking back from time to time with the person in front of him that he has got the message right. In this way the client begins a process of sorting and discriminating too and the hope is that he will thus be able to make sensitive and rational decisions about the way ahead. The would-be counsellor who is sure about the way ahead for each client before he starts would perhaps be wise not to start at all, but if he has a genuine interest in people and knows what he doesn't know, counselling skills can be learned. The practice of any art concerned with people—teaching, management, casework, counselling, psychotherapy—to be effective needs to be firmly grounded on knowledge of the nature of human nature. During the last sixty years scientific studies of human behaviour have revolutionised our thinking on this subject so it is hardly surprising that there have also been profound changes in social work practice. Changes in response to increasing knowledge will continue and counsellors therefore need to be open-minded. Also since they are daily handling basic empirical data about behaviour of all kinds they should, as a body, be research-minded too.

Counsellors[7] do not need to be professional psychologists or psychiatrists but both these professions must be involved in their training. They are concerned with encouraging their clients to examine their attitudes and values and consider how these might be changed. Their work also requires a sensitivity to social changes. Many of the inter-generational differences with which they are often involved spring from changes in the climate of opinion which the young tend to welcome and which older people incline more readily to reject. Reference has already been made to another area in which important changes in social attitudes are taking place: that of mental illness itself and its treatment. This includes the more serious pathological mental states (the psychoses) in which the patient may be, at times, hallucinated or suffering from insane delusions. At such times he is unaware of his condition, is unable to relate to those around him and the problems of treatment are far from solved. Pinel and Margery Fry threw off the chains and opened the locked doors and today's reformers are now pointing to the prison-like constraints of the institution itself, however well administered. Research workers such as Goffman[8] have made it painfully and abundantly clear that the process of being diagnosed as mentally ill and subsequently treated as a 'mental patient' is to some extent self-fulfilling. If forcibly placed in an institution and stripped of all symbols of our pre-patient identity, who among us, Goffman suggests, would not develop symptoms—of persecution mania for example—which others would diagnose as psychotic. To deny the 'person' in any encounter is to attempt to destroy him and this holds for day to day interactions in the family or the work group; in interviews with counsellors, psychiatrists, social workers and nurses.

In many hospitals attempts are being made to reverse the role of the mental nurse. The custodial system which tends to depersonalise and promote helplessness is being replaced by a situation in which the nurse's function is to respect the person who is his patient, and encourage in him a positive and independent self-image. Already there are former patients, institutionalised over many years, outside the gates and managing to cope with the outside world. This move towards the social acceptance and integration of the odd, eccentric but harmless people in our midst is likely to grow and whereas a book on counselling written only two or three years ago would have dismissed in a sentence the possibility of counsellors being asked to deal with the problems of severely disturbed people, it is now necessary to realise that they may be called upon to do so.

The impact of such changes will be felt most by the close relatives of the discharged patients and it is these people, rather than the patients themselves, who are the more likely to seek the counsellor's help. The change of attitude in the hospitals will have to be followed by a more widespread change among the rest of us and this will hardly happen overnight. Any related educational programme would need to include the offer of counselling help.

REFERENCES

1. Medawar, Peter, *The Art of the Soluble*, Methuen, 1967.
2. Constable, 1965.
3. *Ibid*, p. 2.
4. See Wallis, J. H., *Someone to Turn To*, Routledge and Kegan Paul, 1961.

5. See Report of the Committee on Local Authority and Allied Personal Social Services, Chairman Frederick Seebohm, HMSO, 1968.
6. The masculine gender is used throughout this book in all abstract references to either a counsellor or a client.
7. Here the term is used to include social workers whose task includes counselling.
8. See, for example, Goffman, Erving, *Asylums*, Penguin Books, 1968.

Chapter 2

Theoretical Considerations

In the first chapter we discussed the differences between the three closely related groups of workers—counsellors, social workers and psychotherapists: in this chapter we bring them together again since any psychological theories relevant to one must apply to them all. Halmos, in his inaugural address as Professor of Sociology at University College, Cardiff,[1] groups together those professions (clergy, doctors, nurses, teachers, social workers) 'whose principal function is to bring about changes in the physical and psycho-social personality of the client' as the 'personal service professions' and goes on to discuss their influence on the 'moral reformation' of the other professions (law, accountancy, architecture, engineering) traditionally not so much concerned with personal relationships. In his view the technical training programmes of these others have shown such a progressive growth of 'social psychological tuition originally reserved for the personal service professions' that their professional ideologies are now in a process of merging with what he calls 'the ethics of the counselling ideology of the twentieth century'.

For the purpose of this chapter we will follow Halmos and use the one word 'counsellor' to refer to the members of the personal service professions wherever their work calls for them to play that role, remembering that all of them, except those whose title is simply 'counsellor' have additional roles to play.

Accepting that the success of the counsellor in his job is related to his personal qualities, there must nevertheless be some underlying theoretical structure. Those who scorn the theorists and claim to rely on their 'common sense' or intuition do not behave randomly: their performance is inevitably based on some theory but it is implicit and unexamined. The views of the 'practical man' are based on arguments and assumptions which, because they are unstated, are more liable to error than theories which are more carefully formulated. Burford Stefflre of Michigan discussing this point has written 'The real question then is not whether we shall operate from theory since we have no choice in this matter, but rather what theories shall we use and how shall we use theories. Specifically in a counselling situation when a client says "I hate my mother", the counsellor's reactions are limited only by his biological status. He can slap the client, he can run out of the room, he can jump up and down on his chair, he can reply "It makes you bitter just thinking about her" or he can do any of a number of other things. When he makes a choice among the responses open to him he must act from theory. That is, he must act from some notion as to what the client means by his statement, what his statement means in the life of the client, what the proper goals of counselling are, what the function of the counsellor is, what techniques are successful in moving towards the determined goals, and the other elements which, taken together, constitute for him a theory of counselling'.[2]

Thus we need to ask, and we do so in this chapter, what firm ground the theoreticians and research workers have to offer us for the understanding of what goes on in the encounter between a counsellor and a client.

The attempt to understand ourselves has only just begun and though we can look to the psychologists for illumination, we will not find certainty. The complexities of human nature and the complexities of the possible interactions between individuals make a search for a specific blueprint unrealistic. As with parents rearing their children, or teachers teaching their pupils, there can never be a rigid script for the role of the counsellor. He is an actor, not in the traditional drama, but in modern improvised theatre and he must pick up his cues with skilled sensitivity to the needs of the other participant—his client—and all his behaviour must be highly adaptive and contingent upon the situation as it is perceived moment by moment.

The psychological problems can be attacked from many directions but in this chapter three major areas are singled out as being especially relevant to the counselling situation. They are the psychodynamic theories of Freud, theories about how we learn and thirdly the body of work on perception, social interaction and linguistics which can be classed together as concerned with the process of communication. There is, of course, a massive library of books available in each of these subjects and all that we can hope to do here is to discuss some of the more important topics and so make it possible to look with more objectivity at the counselling process.

Man and his place in nature has been an overriding concern of the philosophers throughout human history but only when the physiologists were able to examine the functions of the sense organs and relate them to mental activity within the brain did rigorous scientific study of human behaviour become possible. In 1879 Wündt at Leipzig, a physiologist who had studied Philosophy, set up the first psychological laboratory. Harvard housed the second one a year or so later under William James,[3] an expert on the nervous system who lectured on physiological psychology. Psychology was at that time treated officially as a branch of Philosophy and in 1880 James changed overnight from being a Professor of Physiology to a Professor of Philosophy without any serious change in his duties. His famous work 'The Principles of Psychology' was published in 1890. It is so beautifully written and so extraordinarily up to date in its general approach that it is still very well worth reading. James has been compared with his novelist brother, Henry, as a man who wrote psychology texts that read like novels while his brother wrote novels that read like psychology texts.

This twin parentage—Philosophy and Physiology—is still evident in the work of Psychologists today.

In the first chapter it was suggested as a working hypothesis that in counselling we are concerned with 'normal' people in distress rather than patients who are sick. What do we mean by 'normal'? Some confusion arises because the word is used in two senses—as a mathematical concept meaning 'average' and as a judgement—to act in an abnormal manner is to act badly. This latter usage is to some extent an expression of a wish, for example, it is normal to be well mannered and abnormal to be rude: we approve the one and disapprove the other. In rearing children we try to suppress behaviour which we dislike even though it arises naturally among most children and encourage behaviour of which we approve however difficult it may be to inculcate in the early years. One of the highlights in my career as a mother was the day I heard myself saying to a five-year-old 'Don't be so childish!'.

Careful, patient observation of the behaviour of babies and young children, with a counting of heads followed by very simple statistical analysis has given us some guide lines—some information about what is 'average' or 'normal' behaviour at each stage of growth. Such studies show how foolish it is, not to say cruel, to expect a child to know how he should behave—say—in an English middle-class household rather than a Japanese one or in a Gypsy caravan, before he has had time to discover his parents' social class. We accept that children have to learn to walk, to wash and dress themselves, to use knives and forks, but there is less appreciation of the fact that behaviour like 'speaking the truth' and not 'stealing' and 'playing fair' also has to be learned. These phrases are meaningless to a very young child and if he is punished for 'telling a lie' when he makes up a story to save his skin (and what is more 'normal'!) he will be unable to grasp what is going on, and will be likely to make up more stories to explain the rejection, since all of us, from the earliest age, are constantly trying to make sense of our surroundings.

The mathematician's concept of the 'norm' of behaviour in any particular direction is unemotive. Like a naturalist recording the occurrence of a particular plant or bird in each geographical location, the psychologist[4] records the kind of behaviour exhibited by a majority of individuals in certain well-defined circumstances. Thus most children of two can manipulate a block of wood between finger and thumb and balance it on another. They can't explain the phrase 'telling the truth' in any logical way until they are well over school age. Psychological testing is based on the concept of normal behaviour in the statistical sense. The 'average' child is a statistical artefact who makes an average score—does the 'normal' thing—on every examinable vector. He is non-existent of course, because every child follows his own developmental dynamic: growing children do not clock in with any exactitude. Thus there is a range of ages within the 'normal band' (i.e. within which —say—nine-tenths of the cases 'conform') when children can be expected to walk or talk, stop sucking their thumbs and wetting their beds, cease having tantrums and begin to reason and so on. To be outside this band in one or two respects is not of serious consequence: it is only when a child has an abnormal rating in several important areas of development that one needs to worry about his chance of growing up to be a normal adult. Suppose nine-tenths of a group of children are considered to be within the normal band, then the remaining tenth who are outside the range are 'abnormal' in the mathematical sense and they will be distributed, half and half, on either side of the 'normal' ones. Thus the child who reads at two and can grasp an arithmetical progression at four is 'abnormal' at one end of the graph and those who argue for special education for the brilliant as well as for the mentally defective are making this point.

The 'norms' of *social* behaviour are a function of the particular society and alter as society alters. It was certainly abnormal to mention the word sex in a social situation when I was young but now . . . ! Having to shift one's idea of the norm several times in a life-time is one of the stresses only too familiar to this generation of adults. It is the *rate* of change which is now different: *one* shift per life-time was perhaps the norm of the past.

Are people who seek counselling help 'abnormal'? The question is an ambiguous one and can be examined in several ways. Recognition that bodily ailments should be and can be treated is almost universal in this country and people who are manifestly ill but refuse to see a doctor are in a minority. Recognition that help is possible during emotional upheavals is not yet widespread but it is growing. So, on a graph of people's acceptance of the idea of counselling, our clients are unusual—abnormal—at the top end. If the question is 'Is emotional stress abnormal?' the answer must clearly be No. To say that emotional ups and downs are inseparable from intimate, personal relationships is tautological—'intimate', 'personal' and 'emotional' being almost synonymous terms. The important question is 'Is it abnormal to be unable to cope with such stresses?' Here we are on uncertain ground. It could be that if our educational system was as much concerned with the exploration of emotional behaviour as it is with cognitive behaviour people would grow up better able to manage their personal affairs. Perhaps if social living changed in the direction of more community living and less isolation in our own separate boxes, counsellors would be using their skill and their concern in a social setting and not in a separate institutional setting. What seems to be certain is that we all need to be accepted as of some worth to somebody, we need to have our feelings respected and we need to be able to talk out our confusions and dilemmas without being judged to be wicked or inadequate. The majority, during the greater part of their time have these needs satisfied but our society is very far from making this a life-long experience for everyone.

Democratic procedures are more difficult and complicated than authoritarian ones and 'freedom' can be frightening.[5] It is easier —safer—to be a chattel or a boss than to maintain a partnership where the possibility of breakdown is so much greater and in civilised societies of the twenty-first century counselling services are therefore likely to be part of the 'normal' provision. In making such a prediction we are assuming not only that democratic procedures are more difficult than the giving and taking of orders, but also that they are universally preferred and that the growth of civilisation is inseparable from the growth of democracy. We are, in fact, as Halmos has pointed out, accepting as our basic ethic the worth of each individual.

FREUD AND THE CONCEPT OF THE UNCONSCIOUS

The early humanitarian philosophers felt that a proposition had only to be stated rationally to be accepted. Freud's basic contribution was to show us that our behaviour is motivated at least as much by our emotional state as by rationality. Actions are decided not only by reason but by our innermost desires and needs.

Freud was born in 1856, fourteen years after William James, in a small town in Moravia which is now part of Czechoslovakia. He studied medicine in Vienna and later, like James, specialised in the physiology of the nervous system. Some years were spent in Paris studying hysteria which, up to that time, had been regarded as a woman's disease associated with disturbances of the uterus. (Hence the name, the Greek word for uterus being hustera.) By the use of hypnosis, Charcot, at the Saltpetrière Hospital in Paris had shown that the problems of the hysteric were connected with psychological disorders and Freud continued to work in this area when he returned to Vienna. 'Studies in Hysteria' by Freud and Breuer was published in 1893. It was Breuer who first encouraged his patients to discuss their emotional problems while under hypnosis, a process for which he used the terms cartharsis or purging, but after the publication of their book the two men went their separate ways and Freud developed the method of free association and dream analysis which are fundamental techniques of psychoanalysis. Thereafter, Freud engaged himself in a long and arduous self-analysis, including the study of his dreams and his book 'The Interpretation of Dreams'[6] is one of the seminal works of this century. In the introductory note, he argues that 'the hysterical phobias, the obsessions, the delusions—must, for practical reasons, claim the attention of the physician. The dream, as we shall see, has no title to such practical importance, but for that very reason its theoretical value as a typical formation is all the greater, and the physician who cannot explain the origin of dream-images will strive in vain to understand the phobias and the obsessive and delusional ideas, or to influence them by therapeutic methods'.[7]

Out of such self-analysis and his studies of patients, he developed the concept of the unconscious which has had an all pervasive influence on our generation. Disciples during his lifetime, such as Adler and Jung, disagreed with him on details and broke away to develop their own systems of therapy. The process continues,[8] but none of this detracts from Freud's unique niche in the history of ideas. In this regard, his revolutionary ideas rank with those of Galileo and of Darwin.

Freud did not, of course, originate the idea of unconscious mental processes. In his struggle towards self-awareness, man, and perhaps especially European man, has tended to split his experience into two aspects—the world of matter outside himself and his awareness of it. This duality arose out of and was, in a sense, forced upon him by the conflict between the world of nature and his own needs and was a necessary stage in the realisation of his own potential. Self-awareness serves the biological function of assisting man to deal with the conflict and thus to remove the condition which provoked the self-awareness. 'Pain and conflict provoke our concentrated attention and difficulties are magnified, while the free play of spontaneous vitality—as in the transitory rhythms of eating, drinking, walking, loving, making things, working well, thinking and dreaming—evokes no persistent differentiated awareness'.[9] When we 'feel right' we are unaware: perfectly co-ordinated complex processes which have made possible the continuity of life over millions of years are a biological commonplace which we take for granted.

Philosophers, poets, mystics and ordinary men and women have always had glimmerings that self-conscious man was not the whole man. We are urged to know ourselves but are intuitively aware of the value of activities in which we can project ourselves. Whyte's book provides an invaluable collection of instances of such insights by writers whom he calls 'The Discoverers' from early Greek and Christian philosophers of A.D. 400 and earlier through St. Thomas Aquinas, Dante, Montaigne to Henry Maudsley whose views, published in 1867, were almost certainly known to Freud.

Many of Whyte's 'discoverers' are household names. In his 'Pensées', Pascal, for example, leaves us in no doubt of his insight into mental activities which lie behind conscious reason. He uses the term 'heart' (coeur) to convey a sense of the inner depths of human nature. 'The heart hath its reasons, which reason knows not' is a famous passage occasionally associated inappropriately with romantic love. Every play of Shakespeare's yields at least one relevant intuitive passage and every reader will have his own favourites.

Othello, Act II

' . . . the thought whereof
Doth, like a poisonous mineral, gnaw my inwards'

Macbeth, Act V

'Canst thou not minister to a mind diseased;
Pluck from the memory of a rooted sorrow;
Raze out the written troubles of the brain;
And with some sweet oblivious antidote
Cleanse the stuff'd bosom of that perilous stuff
Which weighs upon the heart?'

to which the doctor replies:

'Therein the patient
Must minister to himself.'

And finally the famous passage from The Merchant of Venice beginning 'In sooth I know not why I am so sad' and ending

'And such a want-wit sadness makes of me
That I have much ado to know myself.'

Rousseau—controversial figure though he is—has been called the first modern man because of his intense endeavours to understand his own emotional nature. He was born in 1712 and had a profound influence on the Romantic Movement. 'In an important sense he is the visible source of the movement which led to the discovery of the role of will and emotion in the processes that lie below the threshold.'[10] In his 'confessions' Rousseau reflects on his own self-analysis:

'The true and primary motives of the greater part of my actions are not so clear to me as I have for a long time imagined.'

'These experiences have procured for me, by reflection, new light on my self-knowledge, and on the true motives of my conduct in a thousand circumstances on which I have so often deceived myself.'

Ambivalence—the duality of love and hate—is a cornerstone of Freudian theory and a concept of major importance for anyone concerned with problems in human relationships. The ability to love and hate the same object is demonstrated most starkly in the young child's relationship with his parents before he has learned that some suppression of his negative feelings is expected. All the 'good' things of life spring from his parents—food, comfort, protection—and these are also the people who frustrate him. His impulse to power is basic and the adults put an end to many of his attempts to explore the world around him, they confine him in a thousand ways; how is he to know that this is all part of their protectiveness? To him it is a denial of life. Thus he will throw his arms around his mother one moment and kick out at her in a rage the next. Mother may behave in the same way, though, for most of us, the image of the all-loving mother haunts us and frustrations over our children make themselves felt in other ways.

The way in which a child's aggression is handled varies from one society to another and as we in the West know very well, may also vary over time within one society. Some child-rearing practices are very harsh and punitive, others gentle and permissive. Anthropologists are interested to discover exactly how the various methods affect the personality of the mature adult but incontrovertible evidence is elusive since so many other variables are at work during the years of childhood.

It is as well to remind ourselves that a child born without any aggressive impulses, without the will to fight for what he needs is a pitiful sight because he lacks the will to live, and with the normal child the problem is not to extinguish his aggression but to find ways to deal with it constructively. Freud's vision was of 'rational man' able to recognise his ambivalence and the unconscious roots of his feelings of shame, hatred and envy, and so to organise society that a child could grow up to be at peace with his own nature.

Decisions to deny oneself the fulfilment of some 'need' in order the better to achieve some competing goal can of course be made at the conscious level. Those, who, from a religious sense of vocation, deny themselves the pleasure of sex should be urged, (and generally are) to recognise the great value of what they have decided to relinquish. There are pros and cons in all real choice: ambition for money or social position may compete with the desire for children: choosing one job denies one the advantages attached to another. The important thing is to be aware that the situation is not black and white: that in making a choice something of value is inevitably lost.

The married man, sexually satisfied and proud of his children may insist that the 'world' (along with his money) is well lost but his envy of his celibate or childless brother is likely to show itself in a variety of ways, some subtle and some not so subtle. When we are at our most critical we should ask ourselves how far away is envy. It is simple enough to be complimentary and generous-minded about those achievements which offer no threat to our own.

The social climate of Freud's time was authoritarian and puritanical. The family pattern, especially in Central Europe where he was born, was that of the dominant judgemental father and the quiet submissive mother and sexuality was the enemy which had to be wrestled with and conquered in guilty privacy. This at any rate was the situation for most of his patients so it is hardly surprising that he found that repression (denial) of sexual impulses was associated with mental breakdown. Freud's important discovery, however, was not so much that sexual repression (and the distinction between repression and suppression is a crucial one) can 'cause' mental illness, but that if man is to develop whole and not maimed he must recognise the existence of all his major instinctual needs and find some rational and socially acceptable way of dealing with them. He may decide on the (conscious) suppression of one part of his nature the better to promote another but actually to deny its existence (repress it) is to destroy part of himself.

Freud's developmental theories were mainly male centred until towards the end of his life, and it was left to one of his followers, Adler, to break away and examine some of the implications of the concept of unconscious motivation for the female role.

Woman, like man, has sexual drives and an impulse to preserve herself and survive and her psyche finds ways to put her on the map, ways to retain self-esteem. At the unconscious level the prime purpose of all human beings is to survive and remain whole and when some basic need is denied or distorted the psyche is at war with itself. The linking of sexuality with sin produces a profound imbalance as does the relegation of particular groups of citizens to second class status be they women in a man-made society or coloured people in a white society.

Freudian theory developed from the observation and treatment of disturbed patients has had a profound influence on our ideas about the development of normal individuals. An outstanding name in the history and practice of the counselling of students and other 'normal' clients is that of Carl Rogers, Professor of Clinical Psychology now at the University of Wisconsin. His first major work,[11] written when he was at the University of Chicago, was published in 1942. In it he expounds a new theoretical framework for the practice of psychotherapy which is now variously referred to as 'client-centred' or 'non-directive' theory. He is critical of Freud's therapeutic procedures and his 'optimism' about human nature has sometimes been contrasted with Freud's 'pessimism',[12] but his stance is certainly based on concepts we owe to Freud. His new approach to therapy and counselling has, he says, 'roots in many diverse sources' one of which is 'Modern Freudian analysis' (in particular Karen Horney's critical re-evaluation of Freud's point of view.[13]) 'which has at least become sufficiently secure to criticise Freud's therapeutic procedures and to improve on them'.[14] The major differences can be summarised largely in Rogers' own words 'The individual not the problem is the focus'. 'The aim is not to solve one particular problem, but to assist the individual to grow . . . ' 'it relies much more heavily on the individual drive towards growth, health, and adjustment'. ' . . . this newer therapy places greater stress upon the emotional elements, the feeling aspects of the situation, than upon the intellectual aspects.' ' . . . that most maladjustments are not failures in *knowing*, but that knowledge is ineffective because it is blocked by the emotional satisfactions which the individual achieves through his present maladjustments.'

It also 'places greater stress upon the immediate situation than upon the individual's past. The significant emotional patterns of the individual . . . show up just as well in the present adjustment, and even in the counselling hour, as they do in his past history'.

'For purposes of research, for understanding the genetics of human behaviour, past history is very important. For therapy to take place it is not necessarily important'.

'For the first time this approach lays stress upon the therapeutic relationship itself as a growth experience . . . In some respects this may be the most important aspect . . . The discussion is somewhat parallel to the discussion in education as to whether school work is a preparation for life or whether it *is* life. . . . this type of therapy is not a preparation for change, it *is* change.'[15]

Rogers distinguishes three stages in the counselling process: first the person comes for help—which is, of course, an important and responsible step towards being helped—and the counsellor explains that *he* doesn't have the answers but that the counselling situation can help an individual to find his own answers. When expression of feeling about the problem is encouraged it is usually negative feeling—hostility and anxiety. No attempt is made to stop the flow or to criticise and the counsellor responds not to the intellectual content of what is being said but to the feelings underlying the story. This is stage one. The change-over to stage two for which the counsellor must listen, is marked by 'the faint and tentative expressions of the positive impulses which make for growth'. ' . . . this positive expression is one of the most certain and predictable aspects of the whole process. The more violent and deep the negative expressions (provided they are accepted and recognised) the more certain are the positive expressions of love, of social impulses, of fundamental self respect, of desire to be mature.'[16]

Nowhere in his writings does Rogers' optimism display itself more completely than in this passage.

Just as the counsellor does not impede the flow of hostile feelings so, when the change-over takes place, the positive feelings are accepted as normal and natural. If the client is not to be blamed for his expressions of hatred he must not be praised because he is also capable of love. In this way he can learn that such ambivalence is part of the human condition and begin to accept himself as he is. Insight and self-understanding which is the third stage of the counselling process now have a chance to develop. 'I can see now that if I hadn't . . . then . . .' This is the aim of counselling and it is at this point that the counsellor is enjoined to offer words of praise and encouragement to indicate that along this road lies the hope of success.

Since 1942, Rogers has produced many research papers and

several major works[17] in which the possibility of failure is more soberly recognised and the relevance of various factors in the relationship between counsellor and client are carefully examined.

He continues to work as a counsellor and a teacher and his theoretical writings are always enlivened by copious illustrations from his own cases. Motivation is a major interest—as it must be for anyone concerned with changing behaviour—and in recent years he has written critically of the idea of man being driven along by a variety of specific motives—a sex drive, an impulse to power, a hunger motive, and so on. Clearly a great variety of 'seeking' takes place and such differentiation is necessary in order to describe the complexities of behaviour, but Rogers sees all these activities as part of a general characteristic of the living organism which behaves always in the direction of maintaining, enhancing and reproducing itself. This he has called 'The Actualizing Tendency'. The living organism is 'always motivated, is always up to something, always seeking. So I would reaffirm . . . my belief that there is one central source of energy in the human organism; that it is a function of the whole organism rather than of some portion of it; and that it is perhaps best conceptualized as a tendency toward fulfilment, towards actualization, toward the maintenance and enhancement of the organism'.[18] He goes further than this with a statement, which, if substantiated, would provide some sort of answer to the ethical dilemma of the counsellor pinpointed by Halmos.

'In a lifetime of professional effort I have been fascinated by the process of change which sometimes occurs in human beings in the therapeutic relationship when it is, as we say "successful". Individual clients in such a relationship could be described in very general and theoretical terms as moving in the direction of actualization of their potentialities, moving away from rigidity and toward flexibility, moving toward more process living, moving toward autonomy, and the like.' Behavioural changes can be observed, clients become more socially mature and achieve a better sense of their own identity. Rogers emphasises that he is making these generalities about 'enormously diverse specific behaviours, with different meanings for different individuals. Thus, progress toward maturity for one means developing sufficient autonomy to divorce himself from an unsuitable marriage partner; in another it means living more constructively with the partner he has. For one student it means working hard to obtain better grades; for another it means a lessened compulsiveness and a willingness to accept poorer grades. So we must recognise that the generalisations about this process of change are abstractions drawn from a very complex diversified picture. But the nagging question over the years has been what is it that initiates this process? Every therapist knows that it does not occur in each of his clients. What are the conditions, in the client, in the therapist, in the interaction, which are antecedent to this process of change? In trying to formulate hypotheses in regard to this, I believe that there is no substitute for close observation—with as much openness to unexpected facts and possibilities as the observer can bring to bear, with as much laying aside of defensiveness and rigidity as he can achieve. As I continued to observe therapy, the formulation at which I gradually arrived was very different from the views with which I started, though how much defensive inability to see the facts is still involved no man can say of himself. At any rate, the theoretical position to which I came hypothesised that the process of change was initiated primarily by the psychological climate created by the therapist, and not by his techniques, his therapeutic orientation, or his scholarly knowledge of personality dynamics.'

Rogers' theorising is firmly based on research findings as he has subjected his client-centred procedures to massive investigations and stimulated and inspired many other research workers to 'tease out'—his own phrase—those aspects of counsellor behaviour which relate to change of behaviour in their clients.[19]

LEARNING

A counselling or a psychotherapeutic interview is a learning situation: what has to be clarified is what it is that needs to be learned and what techniques aid learning.

In contrast to the lower animals man comes into the world with very few inbuilt unlearned patterns of behaviour. His strength lies in his adaptability to his environment—his ability to learn how to meet it—and also his ability to learn by his mistakes. In short his ability to learn.

There is no succinct neat definition of 'learning'. It can be confused with growth and to define it as 'improvement with practice' is ambiguous since some highly undesirable activities can be learned. Learning to speak, write, operate a lathe, drive a car are obvious and acceptable examples but there are very many other less obvious activities which are learned—prejudices, ideas, inter-personal behaviour and attitudes to, for example, social and religious matters, or education.

Behaviour which changes and matures regularly and without practice is said to develop through maturation and not simply by learning. Thus many physical activities like holding a cup, standing, walking, running, climbing, are only possible at the appropriate stage of physiological maturity though the *style* of performance is often learned by imitation. Many activities develop through an interplay of maturation and learning—learning to speak for example. The vocal apparatus matures but the child learns the language he hears.

Early experimental work which led eventually to the understanding of some of the ways in which learning takes place again sprang from physiological studies. Pavlov, a Russian born in 1849 who became a Nobel Prizeman in 1904, published many research papers on digestion. His famous dogs were his subjects and were used in studies on the secretion of saliva. He noticed that saliva flowed not only when food was visible but when other objects presumably associated with food, came into view. This led him to carry out a careful series of experiments in which the dogs were 'conditioned' to produce saliva at the sound of a bell by presenting the two stimuli (food and bell ringing) together for a period and then the bell alone. He measured the volume of saliva and found it to be related to the number of times the bell and the food appeared together. Thus the reflex action normally produced by food came to be elicited by a sound. Pavlov called the learned response of the salivary glands to this inappropriate stimulus a 'conditional response' which, due to an initial error in translation, is known in English as a 'conditioned response', a difference in meaning which is small but important.

The objective tradition of sciences such as physiology gave rise to a 'school' of psychology known as 'Behaviourism' led by J. B. Watson.[20] Its best known exponent in Britain today is H. J. Eysenck. The conviction the Behaviourists have in common is that a science of psychology must be based upon a study of what is overtly observable—physical stimuli, muscular movements, glandular secretions and the behaviour which follows. They exclude introspection as a legitimate scientific method and partly because of this have tended in the past to prefer to experiment on animals and infants. This however does not apply to Eysenck or the Behaviour Therapists who will be considered later.

An outstanding name in early psychological theorising about learning is that of E. L. Thorndike (1874–1949) who in his later years devoted himself largely to the application of theory to educational practice mainly at Teachers' College, New York. His experimental work[21] was done mainly with (hungry) cats confined in puzzle boxes with food outside. Once the cat could open the latch the food was his. In such experiments the first trials are lengthy with much clawing, biting and dashing about until the latch is finally moved. The time taken gradually grows shorter with succeeding trials. This is 'trial and error' learning—the cat does not gain any insight into what is happening—it merely learns by the 'stamping in' of correct responses and the 'stamping out' of the incorrect ones. In just such a way does a small child learn how to open a door long before he has any concept of what goes on when he plays with the knob.

Thorndike postulated that the basis of such learning is the association between sense impressions and impulses to action, a system which is now known as the Stimulus–Response (S–R) theory of learning. The importance of his approach is that with the puzzle box it was possible to study the effects on learning of rewards and punishments and of motivation generally. 'Practice without zeal', he said, 'does *not* make perfect.' ' . . . little in human behaviour can be explained by the law of habit; and by the resulting practice, unproductive or extremely wasteful forms of drill are encouraged.'[22]

It was he who started the movement to banish drill from the schools. It is interesting that now that we have a clearer idea of the various methods of learning teachers can keep an open mind about the value of simple conditioning processes for the learning of some basic items of information like tables and spelling. The rote learning of the past was so often associated with punitive attitudes but as small children continually demonstrate, repetition can be fun.

The ability to carry out certain activities automatically like reading, reckoning, washing and dressing and a hundred and one other day to day tasks without 'paying attention' or 'thinking about them' is highly advantageous: one can speculate that the development of the higher thought processes depended on it. As Aldous Huxley[23] has suggested, the function of the brain may not be so much to deal with all the stimuli with which we are surrounded but to shut most of them off so that attention can be concentrated on particular items. Certainly we only 'register' a small proportion of the stimuli which are available to us and can perform routine tasks without retaining a trace of the sight, feel or sound of them. How often do we have to retrace our steps to see whether we have shut the door or turned off the light?

Learning theorists distinguish two kinds of conditioning—classical conditioning as in Pavlov's experiments in which the 'experimenter' (or 'society') controls the stimuli and conditioned responses are acquired. The other type is known as 'operant' or 'instrumental' conditioning and here the subject (animal or human) is free to respond to stimuli in his own way and the 'experimenter' (or parent or teacher) rewards the response he wishes to be learned every time it occurs.

The process of reward is said to 'reinforce' the 'correct' response and so ensure that it will go on recurring, whereas absence of reward extinguishes it. The results of experiments involving 'punishment' as a negative reinforcement, often in the case of animals, an electric shock, are not clear cut. Where an experiment offers a choice between two behaviours an animal learns the 'correct' response more quickly if that is rewarded and the incorrect one is punished. In other cases, where the escape into rewarded activity is not so obvious, punishment can give rise to anxiety and confusion and a general lessening of activity, and so deter learning rather than encourage it. In real life situations punishment of a child (and this term does not necessarily mean cruelty or physical force—a frown of displeasure may be 'punishing' in the language of learning theory) is often not explicit enough—he may not be at all clear which particular item of his behaviour is under attack.

Experimental results suggest that responses can be eliminated more quickly without the use of punishment. Permanent weakening of a response occurs if it is not reinforced. But the weakening process may be prevented if punishment suppresses the response. This is in line with the clinical finding that if a child is allowed to express his aggression without disapproval then there is a hope of redirecting it. In counselling it is postulated that the neutral acceptance of aggression allows the client to discover the intensity of his own feelings and makes it more likely that he will be able to redirect them in a constructive way.

Inconsistency over rewards and punishment (either on the part of an experimenter or a parent or teacher) confuses the situation and with animals 'neurotic' behaviour states can be produced artificially by first conditioning them to expect a reward for certain behaviour—lifting the lid of a box to find food for example—and then making random changes: food one time, and electric shock the next so that the creature 'doesn't know where he is'.

Confusion can arise over rewards also. B. F. Skinner of Harvard[24] is universally known for his work on operant conditioning. He uses mainly pigeons in specially constructed boxes and by carefully watching and feeding at the appropriate moment (by means of a remote control switch) he has his pigeons walking on tip-toe or in a figure of eight or pecking at a square of a particular colour on the side of the cage. Occasionally in such experiments accidental reinforcement can occur. A monkey in a puzzle box may be scratching his head when he presses a lever. If food appears he may associate the scratching with its arrival and be seen busily scratching as if this were an essential part of the business of obtaining a reward. Skinner has called this 'superstitious' behaviour and indeed he sees analogies with human activity in most of his experimental results.

Both types of conditioning play a part in human development. The child has imperative needs for which he must seek satisfaction and society has certain needs to which the child must be conditioned, as far as possible, to respond. Our search for satisfaction operates by trial and error responses mediated by the pleasure/pain principle: we become socialised by having conditioned responses of restraint and consideration for other people's needs superimposed upon the egocentric responses of infancy.

From the earliest years parents and other adults respond to the child's exploration either with approval, indifference or disapproval. Each type of 'feedback' has its own effect. Actions which are approved of become habitual: those which evoke no reaction in the adult may lose interest for the child also or, on the other hand, may prove to be satisfying in themselves (like mud pies and water play) and have no need of reinforcement by adult approval. They can then continue in an emotionally neutral atmosphere and be dropped by the child when they have served his purpose. Disapproval can have varying effects depending upon the emotional overtones and how essential to the child is the activity which is attacked. It is hardly necessary to add that adults vary enormously both within themselves according to mood and between themselves over the behaviour which meets with their approval. Children brought up in homes where their curiosity and play is a nuisance, inhabit a different world from those whose exploration and endless questioning is welcomed and encouraged.

Attitudes to learning and to rationality are thus laid down early in life and determine the sort of adult explorations and learning which 'make sense' to us in our particular situation and thus act as their own reward. This applies whether we decide to study Shakespeare or to learn to pick a lock.

The process of becoming socialised is not necessarily pleasurable but is none the less essential. To survive, a child must be conditioned to become alert and anxious on the receipt of certain stimuli and society tries also to make us afraid to commit anti-social acts. In this it is not one hundred per cent successful.

The two kinds of process go on simultaneously and often overlap so there is danger in making too rigid a demarcation line but it is helpful to make some broad distinction between simple conditioning which is not a conscious process and learning which can be.

In so far as classical conditioning is concerned mainly with physical responses the term 'training' is more appropriate than 'learning'. For example, in the acquisition of physical skills it is the muscles and the hand/eye co-ordination which are conditioned and in acquiring the automatic responses needed for self-preservation it is the sympathetic nervous system which is involved. Conditioning takes place not only in relation to the physical world but in relation to other people, especially in the early years between a child and its parents. We come to react with fear to stimuli which arouse a parent to fear and this can continue into adult life. Most of us are aware of situations that produce in us a state of anxiety—goose flesh appears and the adrenalin flows—which on reflection is seen to be a response which in the circumstances is irrational and useless. Indeed for too many people life is seriously inhibited by a whole series of conditioned responses acquired in growing up alongside inhibited and frightened parents. 'Operant' conditioning on the other hand is concerned mainly with behavioural responses and is more akin to what we mean by 'learning'. Animal psychologists do not usually stay with their animals throughout life. Just as Thorndike deduced from his experiments with cats and puzzle boxes something relevant to the training of teachers, Skinner has been taught by his pigeons how to make a teaching machine. The programming of learning, which is now so familiar to us, so that the learner can teach himself, stems directly from Skinner's work on operant conditioning—the 'rewarding' of the right responses (correct: move on to the next frame) and the 'punishing' of the incorrect ones (incorrect: go back to frame 2). The words 'rewarding' and 'punishing' need their inverted commas to remind us that the whole operation stands or falls according to whether the users of these devices actually find such admonitions pleasant or painful.

In practical terms teaching machines can make certain basic types of learning much more efficient: no false answers escape the notice of the teacher/machine and in addition what 'punishment' is 'deserved' takes place in private. Also a reluctant learner may be beguiled into a learning situation by the irrelevant reward of having a new gadget to play with. BUT, in the last resort, the machines cannot of themselves overcome a stubborn resistance to learning, whereas a human relationship might.

Anti-social, anti-intellectual and over-aggressive behaviour can be seen as the result of learning to undervalue the self. A child in order to survive has to relate to the others in his young life and rely on them. If he is to learn to think of himself as a person of some worth they must convey this to him by their actions. Because of his own needs he will make naturally outgoing gestures and most adults—happily—have an equally natural impulse to respond to the outstretched arms and the trust implied. It has sometimes been called—inappropriately—the maternal instinct. It is not sex-linked: both men and women have very strong innate protective impulses—the sex differences, in so far as there are any, are socially determined. In our society there is—or has been—something of a taboo on tenderness in the upbringing of the male.

Unhappily some children are born to parents who are unable to respond protectively and lovingly to their offspring. They may give them the wherewithal to survive physically but so starve them emotionally that they come to have a very poor opinion of their own worth, a situation which they make bearable by acting out their frustrations either on themselves or on some one or some thing else. The person who commits suicide or suffers from melancholia is just as anti-social as the psychopathic thief or destroyer—the one is blaming and punishing himself for his worthlessness, the other punishing parents and society generally for their failure to value him.

The behaviour therapists maintain that if early conditioning and learning has produced behaviour which proves either undesirable to ourselves or to the law it can be changed by designing suitable situations for stamping out one kind of response and feeding in a more desirable one.

They claim considerable success: indeed Eysenck maintains that they are far more successful than those who use talking cures. Undesirable behaviour can, theoretically, be extinguished by punishment each time it occurs or by rewards for its non-occurrence. Both methods are used by Behaviour Therapists, the one known as aversion therapy in which the model is classical conditioning and the other is a form of instrumental or operant conditioning. Bed wetting was one of the first problems to be successfully tackled by aversion therapy. It is assumed that the growing child is gradually conditioned to the use of a pot and learns that failure to use it appropriately is frowned upon. For the majority of children conditioning is complete well before they go to school, but the rest present a problem. The psychodynamic school of thought concentrates more on the why? Why this child in this home? What does the child 'gain' by it? Much needed attention and fuss? Arousing a parent to anger is better than being ignored? The behaviourist regards these questions as scientifically insoluble, and concentrates on the symptom and how to remove it. The Freudians say this is useless, another symptom will take its place and they will then have—perhaps—a nail biter to cure. In this it would seem they can be wrong—there are many records of reconditioning, apparently without such side-effects.

In the case of enuresis the 'patient' on going to bed is fitted with a pad and electric device which gives him a mild shock or rings a bell at the first sign of moisture. At which (if he is well motivated to be cured) he gets up and avoids an 'accident'. In time the moisture alone will rouse him and he is correctly conditioned like the rest of us. Other types of behaviour which are now being treated by such methods are male homosexuality, alcoholism, transvestism and various types of phobia. The patients are 'punished' by an electric shock when looking at a male nude which ceases when they turn the picture to a female figure; or the shock is applied when the male has put on female garments and switched off as soon as he discards them. The alcoholic is given an emetic with his drink.

To undergo such unpleasant experiences the 'patient' must, needless to say, be a willing victim. This is likely to be the case when the social or family problems arising from the abnormality outweigh its satisfactions. Some people with a homosexual tendency have heterosexual relationships as well and may even be married. Alcoholics in their most sober moments may long for a cure, and those with extreme anxiety states may feel that the cure, however unpleasant, is probably better than the disease.

The ethics of this type of treatment are a matter of controversy though it is arguable that it is no different in principle from the conditioning that society attempts to impose on all its citizens. One difference in practice is that those who apply the laws of learning consistently and scientifically are more successful. Conditioning the young at home or school is as yet a fairly hit or miss affair because the reinforcing agents are human, erratic and not always vigilant. Furthermore there is no agreement about how much conditioning of this kind is desirable nor about what we want it to produce. Few of us want robots though we nevertheless would like people to conform to *our* norms of respectability. Non-conformers are O.K. if we agree with them. This is one of the battle grounds of education: how far we want to involve the learner at every possible stage of the educational process or how far we want society to tighten the screw, which in the last resort is a battle between those who want a fully democratic society (so mistakenly referred to as 'permissive' by those who disapprove) and those who favour a more authoritarian one. This, however, is a philosophical and political issue and has nothing to do with learning theory. Society—the public—decides what children *should* learn and the theorist will advise on how best to achieve results. Children can be taught that they are free to think for themselves or that they must conform to official views: in such issues the psychologist qua scientist is neutral. How far he and other scientific specialists *should* be neutral is yet another ethical issue.

The immediate problem with regard to behaviour therapy is to ensure that the methods are used only on willing patients. What safeguards are there to prevent their use with prisoners—say—or those in mental institutions? In what circumstances if any could this ever be justified?

Operant conditioning techniques for the elimination of undesirable and difficult behaviour in children or mental patients follow Skinner's method of training his pigeons. That is to say the nurse or teacher observes the natural, freely occurring behaviour and rewards those actions which it is desired to reinforce and ignores the unpleasant ones. To carry this out meticulously over a long period of time requires patience and dedication but there is considerable evidence of success. In some cases negative incentives are used, exemplified by the familiar situation of removing the child in tantrums to a room on his own and rewarding him with attention and social contacts when the unpleasant behaviour ceases. The difference between this everyday occurrence and something called treatment lies in the severity of the cases for which outside help is sought and the energy and concentration needed to carry out the systematic regime which acute cases require. One aspect of the problem which is easily missed in the normal home situation is that parents may be unwittingly rewarding their screaming child. The expert therapist would first want to identify what the child finds rewarding before deciding what is most likely to reinforce desirable behaviour.

A third and particularly successful form of behaviour therapy used to eliminate anxiety is called 'Desensitisation'. The patient with a phobia—say an excessive fear of spiders is presented seriatim with a hierarchy of situations involving the presence of spiders starting with the least fearsome and working up gradually to the most terrifying, e.g. actually handling the creatures. This 'treatment' takes place under relaxed conditions: the patient reclines in comfort and may have his favourite music played to him. The importance of relaxation in counteracting anxiety is well recognised and some training in relaxation is an essential part of the desensitisation process. Suggestion also plays a part: the therapist's voice is calm and soothing, he keeps up a constant verbal contact with the patient, encouraging and reassuring. The situations can be actual events, or presented in pictures or, more usually nowadays, the patient is asked to imagine them. In such a situation the anxiety is reduced so that eventually he is able to work through the whole hierarchy and be able to imagine himself

—say—in contact with a spider without any effect on his pulse. Children growing up go through this same process (in a less intense and dramatic form) many times. Fear of the unknown, of strange faces or strange animals is conquered in the presence of a reassuring adult who is patient and allows the initial approaches to be slow and tentative.

We have dealt so far with stimulus—response theories of learning but in all except the simplest physiological conditioning situations the learning organism intervenes. An overfed cat might well settle down in his puzzle box and go to sleep: food only acts as a stimulus to respond if the cat wants it. So our stimulus-response $S \rightarrow R$[24] formula should read $S \rightarrow O \rightarrow R$ indicating that we are not dealing with automata but dynamic organisms who are involved in what happens to them.

Problem-solving behaviour is recognisably different from trial and error learning and is generally called 'insightful' learning. The repertoire of rewards which motivate the lower animals to solve problems is limited and largely physiological but when we reach the primates we find them indulging in exploratory behaviour not unlike that of young children.

Adult learners intervene in a thousand ways between stimulus and response. As the stimuli arrive we organise them and structure them into patterns which make sense to us. Where the information is incomplete such as a word with a letter missing or a snippet of gossip only half heard we fill in the gaps according to our own prejudices and emotional attitudes which are themselves responses learned in earlier years. Thus earlier learning interferes with or enhances later efforts.

In an important series of experiments with apes carried out on the island of Tenerife a German psychologist Wolfgang Köhler devised situations in which the animal could not reach the desired goal (an apple or a banana) directly but had to make a detour or construct some sort of tool.[25] A banana was attached as a lure to the top of the cage and could only be reached by climbing upon and jumping from a box placed in the cage. Only Sultan (Köhler's most intelligent ape) solved it without assistance. Others copied him once they saw how he did it. In another series short sticks which could if necessary be joined together were available in the cage and food was placed outside. Köhler was interested in learning through insight and records the behaviour of his animals with great care. The animal first plays with the stick in a haphazard fashion but he is beginning to 'see' what needs to be done. He may throw the stick at the banana and lose it but he finally manages to use the stick to draw the fruit within his reach. Once this insight is achieved it is repeated promptly on all subsequent occasions. He has 'learned' how to use his tool. The most dramatic result was the occasion when Sultan managed to fit two sticks together and retrieve food which was too far away for one length. Köhler reports that after trying unsuccessfully for some time Sultan abandoned the effort and was left sitting with the sticks in his possession. For a while he squatted indifferently and then began to play with them carelessly. Then suddenly 'he finds himself holding one rod in either hand in such a way that they lie in a straight line; he pushes the thinner one a little into the opening of the thicker, jumps up and is already on the run towards the railings, to which he has, up to now, half turned his back, and begins to draw the banana towards him with the double stick'.[26] He 'gets the idea', 'sees the point' and has what has been called the 'Aha Experience'.

The difference between Köhler's results and those of the American experiments relates mainly to the choice of the problem to be solved. Rats learning to run a maze have only a small sector apparent to them at any one time: in tool-using situations all aspects of the problem are visible simultaneously. This difference led Bertrand Russell to make the comment that apparently 'animals studied by Americans rush about frantically, with an incredible display of hustle and pep, and at last achieve the desired result by chance. Animals observed by Germans sit still and think, and at last evolve the solution out of their inner consciousness',[27] which suggests that Russell felt that the various results tell us more about the experiments and experimenters than about animal learning.

Insight in animals is rare, in children not so rare and in human adults common. The period before an 'insightful' solution is reached is characterised by a cessation of movement (often after a period of trial and error activity), followed by surveying and inspecting the scene and attending to various details of it. Once solved by this method the response is readily repeated: the learning is complete at once, as distinct from a trial and error situation with no insight, when the clawing and kicking (of the cage, if a cat or of the car, if human) is a feature of each occasion diminishing in length only if the problem is mechanically solvable by that sort of treatment. An important feature of insightful learning is that the solutions can be applied to other situations. Once a chimpanzee has learned that he can reach a banana with a stick he will go seeking something to serve as a stick if there isn't one in sight. The relationships and the generalisations are transferred to another situation. Humans can do more than that. They can verbalise what they have learned and preserve it in writing and so pass it on to the next generation.

In this very short review of what the learning theorists have to teach us it is clear that learning involves the learner consciously or unconsciously and while the teacher can help and in some ways control his progress, the ultimate aim of education is to teach the learner how to programme his own progress.

Learning to understand and have some control over one's emotional life is a particularly complex process, since it involves the emotional interactions of the teacher (counsellor) and learner (client) much more intensely than in the usual teacher/pupil situation. However, if there are any established laws governing the way we learn they must have some relevance to even the most complex processes. It is one of the first principles of science that we should not use two hypotheses where one will do, so the attempt to see how far learning theory can take us in an analysis of counselling procedures is perfectly justifiable. This is precisely what the behaviour therapists have done but even in these cases the personal-relation component between doctor and patient also plays a part. The motivation clearly must be strong enough to overcome distaste for the unpleasantness of the treatment and there must clearly be some persuasion and reassurance on the part of the therapist. H. R. Beech, who has done important work in this field with neurotic disorders including stuttering and writer's cramp, makes this clear in a short chapter 'Preliminaries to treatment' in his excellent book 'Changing Man's Behaviour'.[28] Dr Beech's sober appraisal of what is offered by the 'rival therapy "camps"' takes some of the steam out of the conflict, indicates the common ground and goes so far as to suggest that 'the future could well show that elements of both kinds of treatment are worth preservation, and that the best results are obtained when they are combined into a single treatment regime'.[29]

The analysis of a counsellor's job in behavioural terms is rather more difficult because we are nearly always dealing with diffuse problems, not specific ones, and the definition of a 'cure' is pretty elusive. However, this need not prevent us from trying.

A client in approaching a counsellor is 'saying' in effect 'Advise me; tell me what to do'; he is wanting—often desperately—to bring about some change in his circumstances. He is likely at the same time to be sceptical about the possibility of being helped and may expect rejection and hostility such as he feels he has received from other people. Indeed he is quite likely to feel that it is the other chap who must change and to be unaware that he himself needs to do some learning if he is to find any relief from his problem. The counsellor therefore has some important messages to communicate to him at the outset; (a) that he is powerless to change an absent wife, husband, colleague, teacher, lecturer or offspring, but that (b) the client might learn to handle the situation differently and that (c) counselling can help him to do this. Along with this message, however formulated (and every counsellor will find his own authentic way of doing this—there is no blueprint), an additional item of information is essential. From the moment the client enters the premises he must learn that here no one is going to quarrel with him, no one is going to condemn him and that he is going to be accepted in his own right as a person worthy of help. Research results support the experience of therapists and counsellors that a warm, sympathetic acceptance by another person is a fundamental prerequisite if a person in trouble is to feel secure enough to discuss his most intimate affairs and gain some insight into his problems.

Some degree of rapport of this kind is necessary in any relationship, but in counselling it is crucial. The methods of establishing a personal relationship between two people cannot, by definition, be open to the prying eye of an experimental psychologist, so we have to make do with the voice of experience. Such recommendations would include a friendly, positive approach, a smile and some eye contact, no social barriers, a display of sympathetic interest, careful listening, a relaxed atmosphere implying that plenty of time is available and adopting the client's 'terminology, conventions and generally meeting him on his own ground'.[30]

Thus the scene is set: the client has need of help and is therefore motivated to learn. He is now asked to talk about himself. With some people, who may perhaps arrive on the doorstep in tears without an appointment, all this preliminary canter taking two or three pages to describe, may be telescoped into the first few seconds of the encounter. The story may be poured out first—he is clearly taking the warm acceptance for granted—and any distorted expectations he may have about the counsellor's ability to help will have to be sorted out afterwards. If communication begins as a one-way process some back tracking will probably be necessary. I have resisted the temptation to say 'essential' because not a few clients who come to counselling rooms spend the time communicating with themselves and then thank the counsellor very sincerely for his help. Quite rightly: they need a listener in order to verbalise their problems out loud which is quite different from thinking about them internally and this the counsellor has provided. Some clients having heard how they feel can then manage to decide what to do without further outside help. One example of this known to me occurred with a married couple who came together. At least the counsellor *inferred* that they were married; she had to fall back on guess work most of the time. The man was Polish and his wife German and they talked to each other in French and to the counsellor in completely inadequate English. They had four 'interviews'—the first very noisy and tearful—clearly there was a violent row going on. The atmosphere became successively calmer and the counsellor decided that at least part of their quarrel was about the pros and cons of emigrating to Canada. On the fourth visit they arrived bearing a personal gift, arm in arm, all smiles and displaying their one-way tickets across the Atlantic. The counsellor felt that she must accept the gift rather than attempt the impossible task of explaining her professional reluctance. 'I decided that on this occasion it was better to receive than to give; I cannot report what happened during the interviews because I have no idea but they clearly felt that my help had been invaluable.' In this case of course the couple had communicated with each other but had apparently needed an audience in order to do so.

To resume: the client is asked to talk about himself. When we do this in a social context our companion will pick up items from our story which interest him, make a few polite remarks and then probably change the subject. What he will almost certainly not do is pursue any revealing nuances, question us further on embarrassing topics or tell us what he really thinks about us and our conversation. Few adults hesitate to tell children what they think of them, but feedback to adult companions, certainly of a negative kind, is not 'done'. The counsellor's role is not that of the polite social companion so he must listen for and pick up signs indicating areas of stress which seem to be too painful and embarrassing to deal with outright and reinforce the hesitant attempt. Reinforcement is by definition neutral: he must simply be encouraged to stay in the painful area: 'Do I sense that you don't really like your father-in-law? Could you say more about him?' The skill of the counsellor lies in his sensitivity to the client's manner and mode of speech which makes it possible for him to note the important areas and avoid being side tracked into discussion about unrelated matters.

The client is often very ambivalent about the interview—it can be a relief in one sense not to come to grips with what is troubling him—he could go home and decide that nothing could be done about it, that counselling was useless; on the other hand it can be perhaps a greater relief to find someone who is interested enough to discover where his problem lies and help him not to run away from it. Once the client feels able to pursue the topic the

Rogerian—'non-directive'—Hm Hm is often sufficient reinforcement. It conveys—'I'm still here and interested—do go on'. The counsellor must not be afraid of silence: it is the client who needs to do the talking and after an interval the pressure of the silence may help him to do so. A silence, particularly near to the end of the time set for the interview may lead to an explosive, carthartic expression of emotion. There are great advantages in setting a time limit. Dr Johnson's aphorism 'Nothing so concentrates the mind as knowing that you will be executed a week next Tuesday' is apposite. If the client knows that his time is up at twelve o'clock, at ten to twelve the counsellor is likely to hear . . . 'But of course the thing that's *really* bothering me is . . . '

We have been talking about clients who have a need i.e. are strongly motivated, to learn something from the interview. Sometimes 'clients' are 'sent' to us or perhaps over-persuaded to co-operate by a teacher, a spouse or other relative. Such a person is not a client in the accepted sense. His motivation is questionable and may even be negative. He may be very averse to seeking help and have no desire to change his situation. This will become evident at once in answer to the first introductory noises. A husband came after many attempts on the part of his wife to persuade him to see me. To my opening offer 'Perhaps you would like to tell me how you see the problem?' his reply was '*I* don't have a problem, I'm only the naughty boy'. To which I replied, 'But I understand from your wife that you are a works manager with—what is it—a hundred men under you?' The relationship within the marriage having been so clearly defined at the outset he seemed happy to co-operate. The reluctant client must learn at once, as with all clients, that he is not there to be judged, that he might be able to help with his partner's (children's, colleague's) problems and that help is available to him if—and only if—he wants it.

If people are to change their ways there must be a motive—a prospect that the new ways will 'pay off' better than the present ones.

In discussing a client's motives—what he wants from life—what are the things which please and which annoy—the counsellor is frequently led into a discussion of values and, in my experience, often runs away from it. Counsellors have their own insecurities. They are taught that their own views are irrelevant—what matters is how the client feels, how *he* sees the situation. Being a fairly new kind of animal, at least in Britain, their function is not universally understood and they are taunted as being 'do-gooders' or 'middle-class women with time on their hands telling working-class people how to live' or 'of course you don't have any beliefs or standards, do you?' Alternatively counsellors in schools or colleges may be seen as undermining the authority of the rest of the staff.

There is widespread confusion between being 'permissive' (so-called) and 'indifferent'. There is all the difference in the world between the father who allows his adolescent son to say what his religious beliefs are and decide for himself where he stands ethically and morally and the father who doesn't care whether or not he has any. Similarly, for a counsellor to accept that all of us have a system of beliefs and values which influence the way we live is quite different from proselytising his client about his own system. Discussion of the client's way of life and the importance of his value system is part of the counselling process. Very often the values are implicit and need to be discovered and verbalised. The familiar triangular situation of husband, wife and lover often needs to be discussed in such terms. A wife complained that her husband's behaviour was making her ill—she couldn't sleep—was losing weight. He had 'another woman' whom he saw regularly but he still wanted to keep up the facade of his home. 'So I'm nothing but a housekeeper'. She was told that she had of course grounds for divorce which made her angry and when asked why she was so determined to stay with her husband her reply was that she loved her home and didn't want to leave it. This is a familiar story and a very understandable one. In this case the woman came to accept the high value she placed on her home and that her 'flight into illness' over what she had felt to be an insoluble situation damaged no one but herself. She started to lead an independent life under the same roof and produced a much happier atmosphere for her adolescent son. She even began to see that if her husband tired of his paramour his 'new wife' might be a more attractive person than his old one.

To accept the situation in these terms is realistic though some people find it ethically shocking. In fact, she *did* value her comforts and possessions more than her marital relationship: was it not better to sort out her conflict, accept that for the time being her husband would not change and save herself from a very unhappy and neurotic existence.

If the reader will turn back to pages 24–25 he will realise that Carl Rogers' three-stage plan for a counselling interview is completely in line with learning theory. He refuses to reinforce either the positive or the negative feelings—he accepts them as part of human experience and not a matter for either praise or blame. For him the aim of counselling is that the client should know himself better and therefore signs of insight are immediately welcomed.

This is too simple a view of course: there are many other variables which we need not attempt to enumerate. For example, the interview is—one, two—hours out of the client's day and during the rest of it he will be influenced by many other contacts. Furthermore, the counsellor must be the sort of person with whom he can make some rapport so that he cares whether he is praised or blamed. But to think of the client as having various tasks to learn is often a helpful framework in which the counsellor can assess what is going on and appraise his own performance.

COMMUNICATING

The three sections in this chapter are dealing with the same topic—human behaviour: the approach, the terminology, the experimental procedures, in these lie the differences. The kind of learning and the extent of it made possible by speech and the written word puts man in a class apart from the rest of the animal kingdom and makes the learning to use language a very particular form of learning for the human species. Here we will not be discussing animal experiments but observing ourselves.

The maturation of the vocal chords of a baby allows him to start babbling, and the sound of his own voice seems to give him satisfaction since he will repeat the exercise without outside encouragement. When the adult reinforces the experiment by joining in the fun then the child will learn to associate the sound with an object. One of the first sounds is an Mmm sound and it is probably no accident that in most of the main languages, both Romance and Teutonic, the word for mother begins with the letter M.

Thus, in the initial stages words are learned by association, by the simple business of hearing the mother speak them while she points to the appropriate objects. The first picture book is an aid to learning to talk: the child sits on one's knee, turns the pages and produces a response to each picture stimulus which is either reinforced or corrected. Each of our children in turn thought the name for a book was 'no' arising from the fact that we were unrealistic enough to build all our book shelves down to floor level. A young nephew in this early naming stage thought the name of certain flowers was 'no'. It is hardly necessary to add that his mother is a keen gardener.

The stage of fairly submissive conditioning while a minimal vocabulary is built up soon gives way to experimental, creative verbal behaviour when the child chatters ceaselessly and repetitively. He learns the elements of a structure very early. For example, the verb 'gone' is usually one of the earliest to be learned perhaps because the disappearance of a parent is an anxious occasion which has to be faced most days. From 'Daddy gone' the child experiments and invents, producing juxtapositions—cup gone, apple gone and so on—which he has never heard before. Sometimes one of his own inventions will reduce him to helpless laughter. Why, is by no means always clear to the onlooker. Simple conditioning or association won't do as a hypothesis to explain the learning of a language: what we learn is a complex structure, and strategies for handling it, within which we can invent our own statements which follow the rules.[31] At first this is achieved unconsciously.

A young boy well known to me didn't want his father to go to work so came down to breakfast announcing that it was Sunday. ''Fraid it's Wednesday' was the reply. 'No it's not, it's Sunday.' 'No, Wednesday.' This interchange was repeated monotonously several times and finally the child gave in, saying, 'Well it's a Sunday-kind-of-a-Wednesday'—his own creation: a perfectly good sentence and one that he had certainly never heard before.

This power to use words, to invent stories, to think, gives the child a great sense of elation and helps him to identify himself as a person separate from his parents. He can have secrets. One day, he may suddenly say '*You* don't know what I'm thinking, do you?'.

The structure of a language is inevitably related to the cultural structure within which it develops and the language structure in turn is closely connected with the structure of thought. The vocabulary and the ideas are acquired together—they are inseparable and communication between cultures is hampered by this fact. Governments whether at peace or war cannot afford to ignore the findings of the social anthropologists. Geoffrey Gorer, who has done important work in this area, writes in his study of the people of Great Russia, 'The fact that a person has learned Russian as his mother-tongue means that his thoughts and concepts will be limited and defined by the vocabulary and syntax of the language; in certain important ways he will view and interpret the universe differently to the way he would do if he had been brought up with English or Chinese or Esquimaux as his mother-tongue.'[32] He goes on to discuss the psychological effects of swaddling in infancy and the differences between different kinds of swaddling practices. The Great Russians swaddle their babies but release them for feeding: the restraint of swaddling is an impersonal restraint, not associated with the parents as are the frustrations of British children and Gorer quotes as a fact 'that the chief theoretical quarrel between Lenin and Rosa Luxembourg was on the question whether workers could develop "straight" without the tight "swaddling" authority of the Central Committee'.[33]

Our everyday use of the language we learned as a child is largely automatic and the non-literary student often sees the learning of grammar as a complete irrelevance. 'I know how to use words, don't I—why do I need to know they're called nouns?' is the attitude of many young practical engineers. I once found myself in a similar position when a foreign student of English asked me to tell her the rules of punctuation. I was totally unable to do so and had to suggest ignominiously that she submit her examples to me for correction. I *know* how to punctuate—or think I do—but had never and still haven't, consciously formulated any rules.

The process of learning a new subject is partly a process of learning the words to use. A special language, with the meaning of words precisely defined, is essential for the interchange of ideas which the serious study of any subject demands but those in the out-group call it 'jargon'. The uncertain beginner will flaunt his new vocabulary to boost his ego and differentiate himself from the ignorant masses. It is only the highly competent academic, the man who has 'mastered' his subject who will risk his reputation by attempting a translation into simpler terminology in order to communicate with the layman. Those who disapprove call it 'popularising'.

The use of words symbolically—transfer of a term from one context to another, as in the use of the word 'mastered' in the last paragraph—greatly enriches a language and the way in which it can be used to convey nuances of meaning. Tone of voice, emphasis on particular words and all manner of other tricks of speech convey messages not inherent in the words themselves. Communication between two people is thus not restricted to speech: there are always non-verbal cues to be picked up in any encounter. A schoolmaster of my acquaintance years ago had one set piece for those who were given 'lines' for talking in class. 'Speaking is any sign, word or action leading to the distraction of a neighbour'.

We are largely unaware of many signs and strategies we have learned to use in social interaction. Three classes of signs have been distinguished. First there are those which indicate a causal connection between object and sign in the sense that smoke is a sign of fire. With others the notion is one of similarity—maps are signs and are similar to the terrain they designate. A cloudy sky provides information about the state of the weather. In the third class are placed those where the relationship to the object is conventional or arbitrary such as words or mathematical symbols. The non-verbal signals already referred to are bodily signs which fall into the second class. Szasz[34] has called this kind of communication 'protolanguage', the prefix proto meaning earlier or lower, since it is a more primitive form of signalling than that of speech. Such signs he points out have a 'special relevance to the "healing industry" and its patrons'.[35] The senders of the message may be signalling unconsciously and indeed 'communication' is only achieved if the doctor or counsellor is able to recognise that here he is being given a visual indication—part of a map—of his patient's or client's emotional state. Such signs have no specific meaning, they might be regarded as a pictorial representation of a cry for help. They can serve a variety of pragmatic and other purposes. Consider for example the messages that might be conveyed and the varying motives for conveying them, by a fit of weeping.

The recognition of the psychosomatic nature of illness is a recognition of the complex nature of bodily signs. A headache may be not only a symptom of physiological disturbance but a signal for more help and attention.

For cognitive purposes verbal communication is essential but to convey a mood or induce others to pay attention, protolanguage is superior. This is true not only in the psychiatric setting discussed by Szasz but in the areas of representational art, religious ritual, and the dance. In each of these spheres non-verbal means are used to promote highly significant systems of communication.

An interesting and fruitful way of analysing human behaviour, and the one adopted by Szasz, is to take game-playing as a model of the serious business of living. Mead[36] was the first to use this analogy specifically. Man is seen as a rule-follower and a role-taker, and he emphasised that the great interest that children take in games and in learning the rules is crucial for their social development. Anthropology, ethics and sociology are the basic sciences of human action since they are concerned with the values, goals and rules of human behaviour.

The spirit of the game, the belief that the game of life is worth playing Mead called the 'generalised other' i.e. the organised community or group which gives the individual his sense of identity. For a sportsman his team is the 'generalised other' and the social situation in which a person lives is the 'team' for which he 'plays'. This determines who he is and how he acts. The idea has been wittily popularised by Dr Eric Berne in 'Games People Play'.[37] There is no one game of life but an infinite variety. An essential ingredient of any game is a goal of some kind and one aims to win. There are many illustrations in Berne's book of the strategies we employ to gain our ends. 'Since by definition games are based on ulterior transactions they must all have some element of exploitation'.[38] A 'good' game he defines as one which contributes both to the well-being of the other players and to the unfolding of the one who is 'it'. 'Raising' children is primarily a matter of teaching them what games to play and we pick our friends from among those who play the same games.

When two people meet, a mutual assessment goes on and there is some bodily communication whether words are exchanged or not. Each 'places' the other in a hierarchy of his own construction and comes to some conclusion about whether they could 'play' together and whether further meetings would be profitable. The cues are concerned with bodily appearance, dress, physical gestures, what Goffman[39] calls 'facial decorations' and emotional expression. If the voice is heard (quite apart from any verbal communications) a further and important item of information is added. We can be pretty sure about nationality and if it is an English voice meeting an English ear (I explicitly exclude the Scots and Welsh here) we can make a good guess at social class and educational level. A third person witnessing this encounter can, by watching the interaction, appraise the level of the relationship between the two people by observing stance, eye movements, changes in facial expression and the pattern of any verbal exchanges.

Gorer in his study of the Great Russians already mentioned writes:—'I first became aware of the existence of the practice of swaddling among Great Russians not from an interview, but from a discussion in our group of typical Russian gestures and body movements. In the course of this discussion Margaret Mead interpreted the movements of one of the gesticulating Russians (a woman) in a way I had failed to and, turning to her asked, 'X, were you swaddled as a child?' It then developed that all but two of our Russian collaborators (these were children of intellectuals) had been swaddled. It may be of interest to note that, though I failed to interpret the gestures at this meeting, I could, after three months' interviewing, tell at a glance, and with practically no errors, if a Russian had been swaddled as a child: the square set of the shoulders, the 'resting position' of the upper arms against the side of the body, further back than is habitual with people who have not been swaddled, and many symmetrical gestures with the forearms and hands, the upper arms being kept in the resting position—these are the chief indicators of which I am conscious.'[40]

The psychologist is interested to discover what 'drives' people to interact with others—what are our motives when we engage in conversation with others, what needs are being satisfied? Argyle[41] lists seven—enough to account for the kinds of relationships which are easily recognised. They are:—

Biological—non-social needs, food, drink, money, etc.

Dependency—the need for help, acceptance, protection.

Affiliation—physical proximity, eye-contact, warm and friendly responses.

Dominance—responses, acceptance as a leader, deference from others.

Sex—bodily contact, intimacy.

Aggression—to harm others, physically or verbally or in other ways.

Self-Esteem and Ego-Identity—for other people to make approving responses and to accept the self-image as valid.

This latter need could explain why most of us tolerate and some appear even to enjoy the many social encounters that happen unplanned in the street, in trains and buses or at work. People vary a great deal in their apparent need for this kind of reinforcement. Those with a view of themselves as friendly and kind-to-everyone will welcome and even seek opportunities to have their self-image endorsed: the withdrawn and introverted with no great inner need for the approval of people they don't know, will be content to sit in silence. Indeed silence and absence of interaction with strangers has been thought by foreigners to be a national characteristic of the British, the stereotype of the American being the exact opposite. It is probably more a class difference than a national one and in any case the mode can change from one generation to another. It could be that because we British can no longer claim to be citizens of a great Empire we feel a greater need for reassurance about our identity and are readier to be friendly to foreigners.

If we were to attempt to list the qualities needed in a counsellor, an ability to communicate would clearly be among the essentials. Since communication is a two-way process this implies the ability to listen, to hear, to perceive what the client is saying as well as reciprocating with a clear message which the client can in his turn perceive.

The verb to 'perceive' perhaps needs definition. Many philosophical works have been devoted to the sense organs and particularly to vision and to the relationship between the light reflected on the retina of the eye and what we 'see'. Thomas Reid, a Scottish philosopher, in a book written in 1764, 'Enquiry into the Human Mind', was the first to use the word 'perception' in the precise sense in which it is used by present-day psychologists—to indicate the mental process by which the mind becomes conscious of an external object. Sensations are the stimuli—light waves, sound waves and so on—received by the senses: perception is the mental completion of a sensation.

Objects reflecting light make a flat pattern of light, shade and colour on the retina which reaches the brain as a pattern of nerve impulses but what we 'see' is a solid object. Viewed from different angles the pattern varies but we learn to recognise them as different views of the same object. Every perception is an acquired perception. Infants go through a long education of the eye and ear before they can perceive what adults perceive and recent work on people with dyslexia (commonly but incorrectly called word blindness) suggests that their brains structure sensations differently from the majority of human brains and that consequently their perception of the ordering of letters in a word or the shape of individual letters is different. The need to educate a baby's ear is particularly obvious: all sounds are at first alarming and it takes time for the child to become familiar and therefore less anxious, with the sensation of noise and to associate the sound with its source. It is easy enough to demonstrate that the education of the senses of adults is incomplete. Two-dimensional photographs of familiar objects taken from unusual angles—end-on views of bananas or ink-wells for example—are a well-known party game.

There have been numerous experiments on the effects of motivation and anxiety on the perception of words and objects, and on the influence of prejudice and suggestion on our perceptions of other people of—say a different social class or race. With many subjects there is delay in the perception of taboo words and other emotionally charged material related to sex or aggression, an effect which is interpreted as being due to inhibition and labelled 'perceptual defence' by the experimenters. Other experiments show that we do not need to be attending or even to be consciously aware in order to perceive objects or events and most of us have had experiences of this in everyday life. We hear someone speak but fail to 'hear' what is said and ask for a repetition: in the interval of time we find it possible to retrieve the message and to discover that we had perceived it subliminally.

Thus our senses cannot be thought of simply as recording devices: the unit of knowledge said Reid is a 'judgment'. Our perceptions are based of course on actual cues from the outside world but are also influenced by our past experiences, our needs, attitudes and prejudices. The final product is not so much a reflection of the external world as our own individually-fashioned match to this world. Professor M. D. Vernon has summed up the result of work on Perception in these words,[42] 'Perception is by no means always a simple, straightforward, unambiguous process, but is in fact liable to many variations and interruptions. These are caused partly by the great complexity of the perceived field of view as constituted by our normal surroundings; and partly by limitations in the perceptual capacity of the observer. He can view only a small part of his surroundings at any one moment; and even when he scans them deliberately, there is much that he tends to overlook or to perceive incompletely or inaccurately. Undoubtedly during the course of his life he learns to perceive more, and more correctly, especially when he has an interest in so doing or when he has received special training. But the effects of knowledge and experience are in themselves liable to produce selective perception and the funnelling of attention to objectives and events about which special knowledge and experience have been acquired. The consequence is that no two observers may perceive a given scene in exactly the same manner, and that they may disagree considerably as to its nature and contents. The skilled interviewer needs to be aware of such hazards and be able to make some allowances for them.'

If one wants to raise a laugh at the expense of the psychologists—and who doesn't—psychology can be defined as 'the systematic rediscovery of the obvious'. The fact that this statement *does* raise a laugh, at least at the first time of hearing it, means that it contains an element of truth. People have been interacting in pairs or in larger groups since—or one might say *before*—the beginning of history, since the primates share with us the practice of these activities, so it would be surprising if we had not acquired some proficiency in interpreting aspects of these encounters. Recent work on eye contact[43] is a splendid example of systematic rediscovery though as always it has included discovery too. Having enjoyed the joke the main point to be noted is that the rediscovery is *systematic* and while proving the truth of some of our guesses will also demonstrate the falsity of others. We then 'know' in a different way and ignore such knowledge at our peril.

Most of us have a natural distrust of those who do not 'look us in the eye' or 'in the face' and are willing to accept, as honest men, those who do. People who stare at us for periods longer than we judge proper are rather frightening and are 'seen' as wishing to dominate.

The movements of the eye during various kinds of social interaction can be recorded by means of a suitable arrangement of a table, two chairs, a one-way screen and a recording device which can be a camera or an observer pressing buttons. Two people in conversation look at each other in the region of the eyes ('Look' with a capital 'L' is the recognised shorthand for this phrase).

Glances vary from one to seven seconds whereas in visual scanning of objects we rarely look for longer than a third of a second. There is some scanning of various parts of the face but the eyes are the main focus—the rest of the time we look away from each other. While I am looking at you, you are generally looking elsewhere: eye contact between us—i.e. both of us Looking at the same time—usually happens for less than a third of the time, but the pattern of gaze is closely related to the pattern of our speech. We look more often and for longer periods when we're listening than when we're speaking. In speaking we look briefly at the ends of sentences and when I'm about to stop talking, I gaze at you for a longer period. If I don't look at you just before stopping you will be unsure whether I have finished and will take longer to respond and continue the conversation.

It is clear that the eyes are used as a very effective signalling device during social encounters. We all meet people—and we do it ourselves—who look over our shoulders when talking (hoping to spot some one more interesting?). Catching the eye of a waiter or a chairman is tricky since part of their skill lies in not allowing their eyes to be caught until it suits them. If you look away while I am speaking I will know that you are no longer taking much notice of what I am saying. There is more eye contact between people who like each other and the length of it between lovers can prove embarrassing to onlookers. Deliberate Looking with a friendly expression when it occurs between members of the opposite sex—'making eyes'—conveys a message which most of us understand. Prolonged Looking with a hostile expression is also easy to interpret.

Watching facial expression and particularly looking at a person's eyes can give us a great deal of information—feedback—on how they are receiving us and for effective social interaction sensitivity to cues of this kind is essential. We learn such skills intuitively and there is wide variation in performance. No doubt we vary in our *need* for acceptance and approval: the hermit avoids his fellow man and doesn't care and it has been suggested that women have developed greater skill in 'reading faces' because in a man's world they need such ability in order to get their own way.

For those whose professional competence depends in any way on 'getting on' with people, research in this area has provided a useful framework for the analysis of social skills. Whether such knowledge is used to persuade people to buy goods they don't need or to suggest that they make use of our counselling services is a matter of choice. The social scientist is in the same position as the physicist: the latter discovers how to produce nuclear fission and we—society—must decide whether to make bombs or electricity. The experimental psychologist may discover the ways in which people can be influenced and how they learn. Who decides in what direction they should be influenced and what they shall learn? Among psychologists themselves as well as among the general public, there are divisions of opinion: *can* we—at least in some areas—take up a neutral stance and *really* allow people to make their own choices as counsellors try to do and as Carl Rogers argues we can if we adopt his 'client-centred' approach? B. F. Skinner maintains that it is impossible to avoid influencing people—in counselling as well as in the classroom, which means that we must programme our activities with great care.[44] It seems to me that the difficulty is at least partially met if in 'programming' our counselling we take care to 'reward' by all the various signs of approval any movement on the part of a client towards insight into his own involvement in the problem and any sign of self-involvement—'self-actualisation'—in the solving of it. The basic dilemma remains however, especially with those resistant to or incapable of self-examination and it is one which people concerned with education have scarcely begun to tackle. We influence our children of course, without doubt, but no one could suggest we 'programme' it rationally or have much grasp of the unhappy side effects—the things we teach unwittingly—of our inconsistent and inconsequential behaviour towards them. It cannot be too strongly emphasised that a 'rational programme' in the sense implied here does not of necessity exclude fun and spontaneity nor indeed any aspect of our relationship with children which we deem to be desirable. The really challenging message is that the adults as well as the children are bound by the laws of learning. As we behave so the children will learn and there is no escape. As a society, though not necessarily as individuals, we get the young people we deserve.

All the evidence indicates that without good face to face relationships, theoretical knowledge about human behaviour and development is valueless. So: parents should genuinely love their children: teachers must be fair minded and respect the integrity of their pupils and counsellors must 'accept' their clients if they are to help them to have confidence in themselves as persons worthy of help. A tall order: it is hardly surprising that many of us frequently fail. Happily children and even adults are very forgiving if the spirit is suitably humble.

The importance of language and speech to the way in which we perceive one another and for our grasp of what makes us tick was emphasised by Freud particularly in his book 'The Psychopathology of Everyday Life'.[45] He wrote a paper on 'The Psychical Mechanism of Forgetfulness' as early as 1898 in which he describes first the psychological implications not only of the temporarily forgotten word or—more often name—but also of the wrongly remembered. In the book he goes on to discuss slips of the tongue and the unconscious processes which may be involved. The disturbances may be due to a confusion of sounds or an anticipation of later words in the sentence or a perseveration of a previous word but Freud was more interested in those examples which result from influences outside the word and its immediate context and arise out of elements which are not intended to be uttered, the existence of which we are unconscious and learn of only through the actual mistake in speech. A year or two ago I heard a leader of a government, not British, when addressing an audience about his distinguished predecessor refer to him as 'another great man'. Freud lists many examples[46] including an example from The Merchant of Venice in which Shakespeare makes brilliant use of a slip to show Portia's love for Bassanio although she is bound not to declare it:

> . . . I could teach you
> How to choose right, but then I am forsworn;
> So will I never be; so may you miss me;
> But if you do you'll make me wish a sin,

That I have been forsworn. Beshrew your eyes,
They have o'erlooked me, and divided me;
One half of me is yours, the other half yours—
Mine own, I would say; but if mine, then yours,
And so all yours.

Another incident quoted by Freud (most of his examples have had to be translated from the German) comes from a magistrate's notebook and concerns a soldier charged with housebreaking. He said in evidence, 'Up to now I've not been discharged from military *Diebsstellung* so at the moment I'm still in the army'. Diebsstellung would mean literally thief position: what he meant to say was Dienststellung which is the word for (military) service. Freud continues:

'The amusement and derision which such oral slips are certain to evoke at the crucial moment can be taken as evidence against what purports to be the generally accepted convention that a mistake in speaking is a *lapsus linguae* and of no psychological significance. It was no less a person than the German Imperial Chancellor Prince Bulow who protested on these lines in an effort to save the situation when the wording of his speech in defence of his Emperor (in November 1907) was given the opposite meaning by a slip of the tongue. "As for the present, the new epoch of the Emperor Wilhelm II, I can only repeat what I said a year ago, namely, that *it would be unfair and unjust to speak of a coterie of responsible advisers round our Emperor . . .* " (loud cries of "irresponsible") " . . . *Irresponsible advisers.* Forgive the *lapsus linguae.*" (Laughter).'

In detecting the unconscious ideas underlying some of our behaviour the psychoanalyst is not suggesting that the one 'causes' the other but that the one helps us to understand and give meaning to the other. We give ourselves away by the hesitancies in the voice, the forgettings and the slips of the tongue. In a recent essay which should be prescribed reading for any counsellor, Charles Rycroft takes up this point:

' . . . the procedure he engaged in was not the scientific one of elucidating causes but the semantic one of making sense of it. It can indeed be argued that much of Freud's work was really semantic and that he made a revolutionary discovery in semantics, viz that neurotic symptoms are meaningful disguised communications, but that, owing to his scientific training and allegiance, he formulated his findings in the conceptual framework of the physical sciences. In some aspects of his work Freud saw this himself clearly. His most famous work he entitled The "Interpretation" of Dreams not The "Cause" of Dreams and his chapter on symptoms in his Introductory Lectures is called The "Sense" of Symptoms. He was also well aware that many of his ideas had been anticipated by writers and poets rather than by scientists.'[47]

Rycroft goes on to make the point that psychoanalysis is not a causal theory but a semantic one and says that those who insist otherwise lay themselves open to attack from critics like Professor Eysenck 'who see quite clearly that psychoanalysis cannot satisfy the canons of those sciences which are based on the experimental method but who believe that if they can demonstrate its inadequacy as a causal theory, they have proved that it is nonsense'. 'To my mind, one of the merits of the semantic view of analysis is that it completely undercuts the Eysenck-Psychoanalysis controversy by showing that both parties are not only, as Eysenck himself has said, arguing from different premisses but from wrong premisses. On their side the analysts are claiming that analysis is what it is not, and, on his, Eysenck is attacking it for failing to be what it has no need to claim to be. And both parties are assuming that it is only the physical sciences which are intellectually respectable. It is perhaps relevant here, that for very different historical reasons, both psychology and medicine are faculties which suffer from an inferiority complex in relation to science.'[48]

Rycroft regards it as futile to discuss whether the 'cause' of neurosis is to be found in the first three months of life or in the relationship with the mother or the father or the siblings. What we need to do is to concentrate on improving our techniques for getting into communication in the here and now with those who have become alienated for whatever reason. He is prepared to throw overboard a great deal of analytical literature on child rearing. The idea that children should be treated lovingly and humanely does not need either scientific or psychoanalytic backing. Furthermore, no one can be loving to order so that much of the suffering endured by children is unavoidable. Children *are* separated from their parents and 'no parent can guarantee to remain alive for the requisite number of years after becoming one' so, much of the advice is sentimental and perfectionist and may be, on occasion, harmful. Many patients are the offspring of tragedy, not of faulty child-rearing. The claim to understand the *language* of the unconscious is a more modest one than the claim to be able to love their patients better than their parents did.

Thus the counsellor along with the psychotherapist is attempting to learn the private language of his client, to learn the language in which he expresses his suffering so that it can be understood and translated back into ordinary communicable language. This is very much what the linguist does when he goes into a community which speaks an unfamiliar tongue.

This concept of the 'talking cure' as a semantic exercise based on a biological theory of meaning i.e. the interpretation of behaviour in terms of the person that experiences it, makes it possible to give some meaning to the idea of 'skill'. Training can be seen as sensitivity training enabling one to learn the emotive, non-verbal, unconscious language of distress. The vocabulary increases with experience. Superiority lies first in a larger repertoire of language learned from earlier clients, increasing sensitivity to cryptic and disguised utterances, to imagery and styles of thought. Finally it lies in increasing ability to translate these messages back into everyday language which will help the person to accept himself, understand his situation better and find a way to some solution.

REFERENCES

1. *The Personal Service Society*, Cardiff, University of Wales Press, 1965.
2. *Theories of Counselling*, ed. Stefflre, Burford, McGraw-Hill, 1965, Ch. 1 by the Editor 'Function and Present Status of Counselling Theory', p. 3.
3. See Knight, Margaret, *William James*, Penguin Books, 1950.

4. For example Arnold Gesell at the Yale Clinic who studied large numbers of children in the first five years of life. Gesell, Arnold, *The First Five Years of Life*, Harper and Row, 1940.
5. See Fromm, Eric, *The Fear of Freedom*, Routledge and Kegan, Paul, 1942.
6. Authorised translation by A. A. Burell, Allen & Unwin. First published 1913.
7. *Ibid*, p. 15. Third Edition, 1932.
8. *Freud and the Post-Freudians*, J. A. C. Brown, Penguin Books, 1961.
9. *The Unconscious before Freud*, Lancelot Law Whyte, Tavistock, 1962, p. 35.
10. *Ibid*, p. 109.
11. Rogers, Carl R., *Counselling and Psychotherapy*, Houghton Mifflin Company, 1942.
12. Arbuckle, D. S., *Five Philosophical Issues in Counselling*, 'Journal of Counselling Psychology', 1958, **5,** 211–215. (Reprinted in *Counselling Readings in Theory and Practice*, McGowan and Schmidt (eds), Holt Rinehart and Winstone Inc., 1962, p. 107.
13. Horney, Karen, *New Ways in Psychoanalysis*, W. W. Norton & Co., N.Y., 1939.
14. Rogers, *ibid*, p. 28.
15. *Ibid*, parts of pp. 28–30.
16. *Ibid*, p. 39.
17. For example: *Client Centred Therapy*, 1951; *On Becoming a Person*, 1961.
18. Rogers, Carl R., *The Actualizing Tendency in Relation to Motives and Consciousness*, 'Nebraska Symposium on Motivation', University of Nebraska Press, 1963, p. 6.
19. See for example

    Grummon, Donald L., *Client-centred Theory*. Ch. 2 in Stefflre, B. (ed.), *Theories of Counselling*, McGraw-Hill, 1965.

    Truax, C. B., *Elements of Psychotherapy*, Discussion Papers Wisconsin Psychiatric Institute, No. 38, University of Wisconsin, 1962.

Truax, C. B. and Carkhuff, R. R., *Towards Effective Counselling and Psychotherapy*, Chicago, Aldine, 1967.
20. Watson, J. B., *Psychology from the Standpoint of a Behaviourist*, Philadelphia, Lippincott, 1919.
21. Thorndike, E. L., *Animal Intelligence*, N.Y., Macmillan, 1911.
22. Thorndike, E. L., *The Psychology of Learning*, N.Y. Teachers' College, 1913.
23. Huxley, Aldous, *The Doors of Perception* and *Heaven and Hell*, Penguin Books, 1959.
24. See p. 56.
25. Köhler, W., *The Mentality of Apes*, trans. by Ella Winter, N.Y. Harcourt, Brace, 1925, first published in Germany in 1917, re-issued Penguin Books, 1957.
26. *Ibid*, pp. 132–133.
27. Russell, Bertrand, *History of Western Philosophy*, Allen & Unwin, 1946.
28. Beech, H. R., *Changing Man's Behaviour*, Penguin Books, 1969.
29. *Ibid*, p. 258.
30. See Argyle, Michael, *The Psychology of Interpersonal Behaviour*, Penguin Books, 1967, p. 97.
31. Noam Chomsky is the leading name in this field. For an introduction to his work and a bibliography see Lyons, John, *Chomsky*, Fontana Modern Masters Paperback, 1970.
32. Gorer, Geoffrey and Rickman, John, *The People of Great Russia. A psychological study*, Cressel Press, 1949, p. 207.
33. *Ibid*, p. 216–217.
34. Szasz, Thomas S., *The Myth of Mental Illness: Foundation of a Theory of Personal Conduct*, Secker & Warburg, 1961.
35. *Ibid*, p. 117.
36. Mead, George H., *Mind, Self and Society—from the Standpoint of a Social Behaviourist*, University of Chicago Press, 1934.
37. Sub-title *The Psychology of Human Relationships*. First published 1966, Penguin Books, 1970.
38. *Ibid*, p. 163.
39. Goffman, Erving, *Behaviour in Public Places*, The Free Press, N.Y., 1963, p. 33.
40. *Ibid*, p. 211.

41. Argyle, Michael, *ibid*, p 14.
42. Vernon, M. D., *The Psychology of Perception*, Penguin Books, 1962.
43. See Argyle, Michael, (a) *The Psychology of Interpersonal Behaviour*, Penguin, 1967; (b) *Social Interaction*, Methuen, 1969.
44. See *Science and Human Behaviour*, Macmillan, 1953, and also Skinner's novel *Walden Two* in which he invents a Utopia founded upon the Behaviourist approach.
45. Trans. Alan Tyson, paperback edition, Ernest Benn, 1966.
46. *Ibid*, pp. 61–105.
47. *Psychoanalysis Observed*, ed. Charles Rycroft. Introductory essay by the editor entitled *Causes and Meaning*, Paperback, Constable, London, 1966, p. 14.
48. *Ibid*, pp. 14–15.

Chapter 3
Group Counselling

So far we have discussed Counselling and the helping services generally in terms of individuals—of an interaction between the counsellor and a client or the doctor and his patient. However, the influence of a group on its members is well recognised. Parents, anxious for their children to be influenced in the 'right' way want them to go to the 'right' schools and join the 'right' clubs. They worry about 'the company' they keep and try to veto groups whom they think are likely to have a 'bad' effect. Their intuitions about the potential dangers are sound though a desire to isolate a youngster from 'alien' influences may not be. Throughout childhood the influences of peer groups competing with family bonds allow us to explore our own identity and complete the weaning process. As adults we have to be able to 'stand on our own feet' and adolescents need to be helped to cope with the dangers rather than to be kept in blinkers.

It is a distinctively human characteristic to combine together in groups. They come in varying sizes and are set up for varying purposes. We have invented special names for particular kinds. For small ones the name can relate to the actual number involved —a 'pair' or a 'couple', a 'trio', a 'quartet'. There are collective nouns for groups with a definite purpose and function: family, for example; partners in a company; a flock or a congregation; a school, a class or a youth club; a college or seminary; a battalion. These words suggest relationships of varying degrees of intimacy. 'Crowd' conveys greater size and less coherence while 'mob' and 'rabble' move even further from intimacy and nearer to anarchy. Visible signs of membership as part of clothing are frequent, ranging from a ritual tribal costume to old school ties and badges or buttons in profusion.

The promotion of groups as a helping agency is comparatively recent and we now have a wide variety of clubs and societies which bring together people with a common problem—widows, the divorced, the lonely, parents of handicapped children, alcoholics and so on. It is a matter of common observation that members of groups develop a warmth and loyalty towards fellow members which can and frequently does, last a lifetime. Where the group is united by membership of a formal organisation involving either a common faith, a common political ideology or a common expertise, academic or cultural, such fellow feeling can extend to members who are in every other respect strangers and membership of such a body can prove to be an international passport.

A particularly strong bond develops between people thrown together in dangerous situations such as arise in wartime, either among troops or among civilians subject to bombardment. In Germany and Austria there are 'Belsen groups' and 'Auschwitz groups' bringing together survivors of the horrors of those Nazi camps. S. H. Foulkes, the psychiatrist whose name is associated with group therapy, in a paper written in 1946 said:

'. . . A wider view will see in it (group treatment) a new method of therapy, investigation, information, and education. The widest view will look upon group therapy as an expression of a new attitude towards the study and improvement of human inter-relations in our time. It may see in it an instrument, perhaps the first adequate one, for a practicable approach to the key problem of our time: the strained relationship between the individual and the community . . . Perhaps someone taking this broad view will see in it the answer in the spirit of a democratic community to the mass and group handling of totalitarian regimes.'[1]

W. R. Bion, another psychiatrist working with patients in groups wrote his first paper on the subject in 1943[2] based on his experiences in a military psychiatric hospital. He concluded that there was 'a need for further examination of the structure of groups and the interplay of forces within the groups. Psychology and psychopathology have focused attention on the individual often to the exclusion of the social field of which he is a part. There is a useful future in the study of the interplay of the individual and his social group, viewed as equally important interacting elements.'

The social scientists took up Bion's challenge and indeed some of their studies pre-dated him. Weber, one of the founding fathers of sociology, had already set us thinking about styles of leadership, giving names to three types of organisation which everyone can readily recognise. These are the 'paternalistic' with what the psychoanalysts would call a 'father figure' at the head: the 'functional' in which the leader is chosen for his 'know-how', his experience in the business and the 'charismatic' (borrowing the word 'charisma' from the theologians) where the leader is accepted because of the power and attraction of his personality. Members revere him regardless of whether he has had a prior relationship with the organisation or has any prior knowledge of its procedures. Clearly to have as chairman of an organisation a member of the House of Lords who also has the appropriate expertise is the ideal solution!

What later social scientists did was to devise means to examine the observations of Weber and others, objectively, to see how far for example one can demonstrate the nature of the leadership by questioning the members of a group and monitoring their interactions and so go on to relate organisational structure to other variables. They want to be able to say what type of leadership is most effective in what circumstances with what kinds of people.

Social psychologists are basically interested in the behaviour of the individuals within a group and sociologists in their professional capacity tend to regard the group itself as the unit of study. The sociologists are interested in organisations rather than individual men and idiosyncratic managers; in marriage as an institution in varying societies rather than a particular marital partnership. There can be no hard and fast demarcation line between the two fields of study—they obviously overlap considerably—but it is roughly true to say that the sociologist's job is to study *group* behaviour, to determine the nature of the average member, the stereotypical Englishman or German. (The Greek word 'stereos' means solid). The psychologist concentrating on individual behaviour is interested to note how an individual Englishman deviates from the norm, to discover, for example, that he never wears a bowler hat and enjoys singing German lieder.

Here is a statement which expresses some sociological findings.[3]

'The more interaction, the more positive is the sentiment towards others in the group and to those who interact frequently in particular, except:

(a) where interaction does not give information about personalities

(b) where the task is disliked

(c) where interaction does not give information about the sentiments of other members

(d) in two other cases

  (i) where control is attempted by a member with deviating norms

  (ii) where sub-groups have different norms.'

This might perhaps have been written by a philosophical observer of his fellow men sitting in an armchair. We have all experienced the situation—on joining a committee for example—in which one starts critically, thinking perhaps that 'these people' seem rigid or set in their ways or have too high an opinion of their worth or whatever the prejudice might be, only to find after a few months of working together that we now feel that they are a charming bunch whom one is glad to number among one's friends. Checking down the list of findings quoted above we find that we like them (have positive sentiments towards) because we have (a) come to know them as persons (have learnt something about their personalities); (b) have enjoyed the job (the task is liked: that being the reason for joining in the first place); (c) we have discovered how *they* feel about the job too (they have given us information about their sentiments); (d) the few members who don't share the general feelings take very little part (there is no attempt to dominate by any member who disagrees with the majority, i.e. has deviating norms) and finally the group is by and large in agreement about its purposes and methods and there is very little division into factions (sub-groups with different norms).

I have spelled this out in order to emphasise that although we can read these findings and see how they fit our own experience the sociologist has not derived them anecdotally or from his own hunches. Each of the seven statements represents the result of carefully devised experimental groups in which the behaviour of each individual—how many times he spoke, what was said and so on—was painstakingly recorded and his preferences for the others in the group monitored each week by means of questionnaires.

Josephine Klein quotes one such set of questions used to give ratings of the popularity of each member which could then be correlated with the amount and the quality of each individual's communications.

'1. If you found you had left your money at home, from whom would you borrow for the day?
2. Who do you think would be a valuable member on any committee?
3. If you had a spare ticket for a concert, to whom would you offer it first?
4. Different people know different sets of facts; whose total knowledge would you most like to have?
5. If you could read only twenty books for the rest of your life, whom would you prefer to select them for you?
6. If you had to share rooms with someone, whom would you choose?'[4]

In some such tests the questions are framed around *actual* happenings such as 'Who did you in *fact* go with to the concert?' The one quoted is not a test of reality but very little imagination is needed to translate the questions into everyday experiences. In this form subjects can be asked the same questions over and over again and are free to change their minds, so that shifts in the popularity ratings can be recorded.

Kurt Lewin, a German psychologist who spent his last years in the States, propounded a psychological theory known first as 'topological psychology' and later as 'field theory' which has had an important influence on the study of groups as well as on learning theory.

In his Berlin days he was a member of the so-called 'Gestalt'[5] group along with Köhler.[6] They repudiated the idea that we learn simply by association of one thing with another—say the name with the object—or by trial and error. They showed in a variety of demonstrations that we can learn by 'insight': we can 'see' the end to be desired and turn away from it temporarily to find the means to achieve it. This 'detour' character of the performance of Köhler's apes was the important feature of his observations. The 'Gestalt' psychologists' main work was in the field of perception and it was they who drew attention to the problem of visual illusions. The human brain *organises* the sensations which reach it through the eye making of them a 'Gestalt' in which objects are perceived against a ground. Many well-known illusions are percepts in which the object and its ground are interchangeable so that they can be 'seen' and 'organised' in two ways, often appearing to jump from one 'Gestalt' to the other. There is the picture of two Greek vases which can 'become' a face and drawings of staircases or boxes which 'move' in and out according to whether they are perceived apparently from below or from above.[7]

Lewin progressed from these observations to more complex psychological situations and felt a need for a new language in which to 'structure' his findings. He found what he wanted in language derived from geometry and mathematics—terms such as 'topological' and 'vector'. Topology is a non-metrical geometry of space using concepts such as 'inside', 'outside' and 'boundary'. 'Vector' is a term borrowed from the mathematical system used in mechanics to describe the resolution of forces. Unlike topology, vectors are metrical: they imply a force of a certain quantity applied in a certain direction. They are usually represented by arrows in which the length is a measure of its force and the direction the line of its application.

Thus Lewin[8] leads us to think of the psychological fields as the life space in which a person moves—not a physical space but a psychological space—so that two people can be together in physical space but be 'miles' apart psychologically. We can sit at home making plans and 'move' in a different world. My physical and psychological worlds overlap because the people, ideas and things included in my psychological space are a selection—*my* selection—from the total physical world available to me. Interactions with other people produce changes in our psychological worlds. My psychological world is conditioned and influenced by my physical, social and conceptual environment but cannot be identified with it. Lewin spoke of life space as quasi physical, quasi social and quasi conceptual.

The important point to note is that this configuration of a person's life space is not a matter of introspection—we are not always able to discover by introspection what forces are acting upon us at any moment—it is something to be constructed to account for the person's psychological situation at any given point in time. Thus Lewin's writings are interlaced with diagrams in one of which, for example, a point P (the person) is enclosed inside a space (his present home or school) with a succession of spaces attached (also bounded by lines) representing what his future activities must be—college entrance (ce), period in college (c), medical schools (m), internships (i), establishing a practice (pr.)—before he can reach the final space which represents his goal (+G) (Figure 1). This represents the boy's life space at a time when he is wanting to become a physician and is looking at the hurdles. On another occasion his motivation may have weakened and the diagram would have to include vectors (arrows) directed towards the point P—the person—indicating the contrary pressures taking him *away* from the goal.

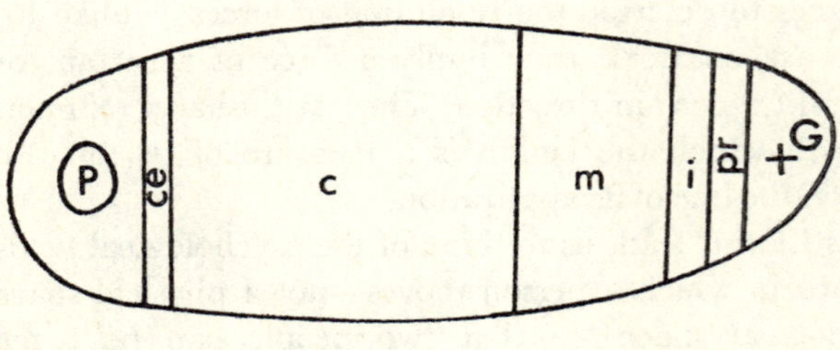

FIGURE 1. Copied from *Principles of Topological Psychology*, K. Lewin, 1936, McGraw-Hill Book Co. Inc.

When the life space corresponds very closely to the real world as does the one just described we can say that this boy is in touch with reality. Other diagrams might show an individual living in a world of fiction quite unlike his physical world.

Lewin's innovation—the invention of a new geometry to fit the problems of psychology—has been much criticised on the grounds that concepts derived from physics are inappropriate and that anyway his mathematical understanding was faulty. However, concepts of movement, force, direction, resolution of conflicts, spaces with boundaries where people can be either outside or in are valuable as an indication of the dynamic nature of psychological events. His idea has been used and modified in a variety of ways and Lewin-type diagrams to indicate the nature of groups are commonplace. In studies of leadership patterns, groups in which the pattern of interaction (as recorded with the help of suitable sociometric questionnaires) is almost entirely between the leader and each individual member are represented in this way:—

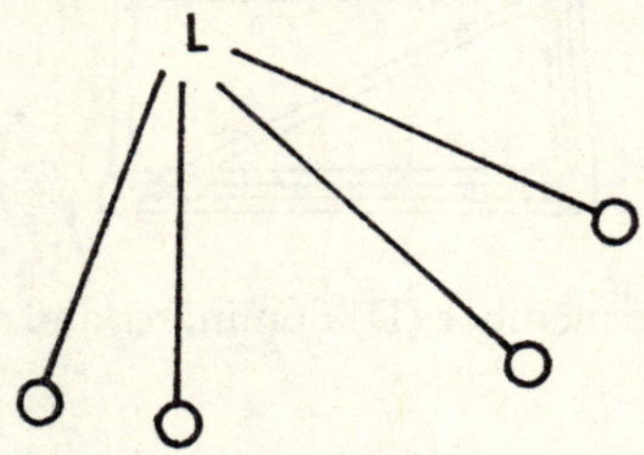

Whereas those in which every individual interacts with every other produces this pattern:—

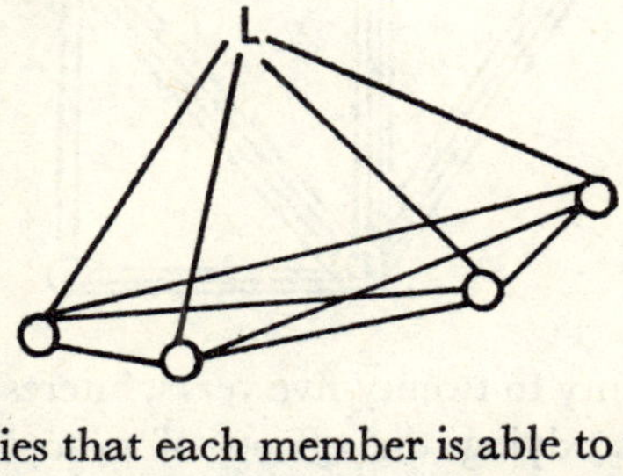

The second implies that each member is able to talk to and listen to each other member—that no member is isolated. There is, in

Lewin's phrase, a factor of 'belongingness' in such a group. The proportionate numbers of communications between individuals can be represented diagrammatically to show, for example, a case of isolation (I):—

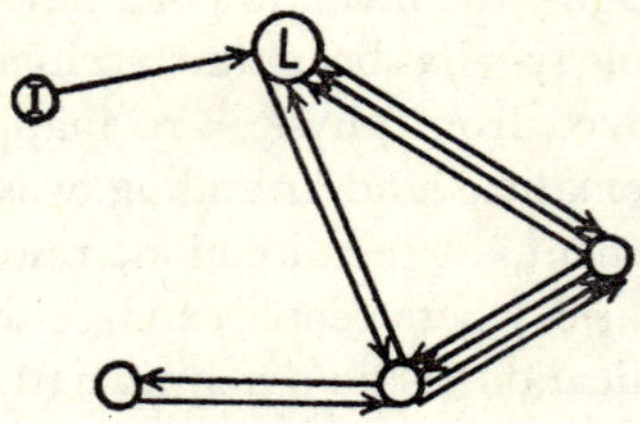

or the formation of sub-groups:—

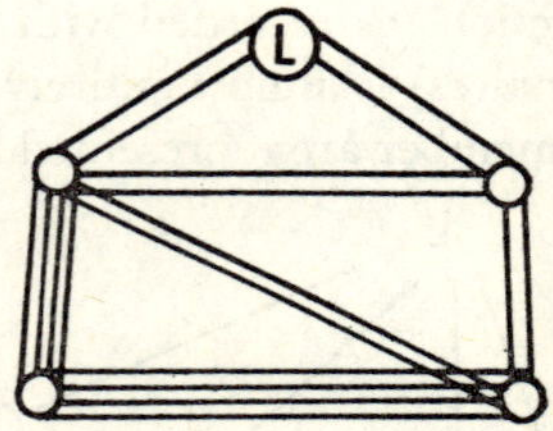

or a case where one member (D) dominates and competes with the leader:—

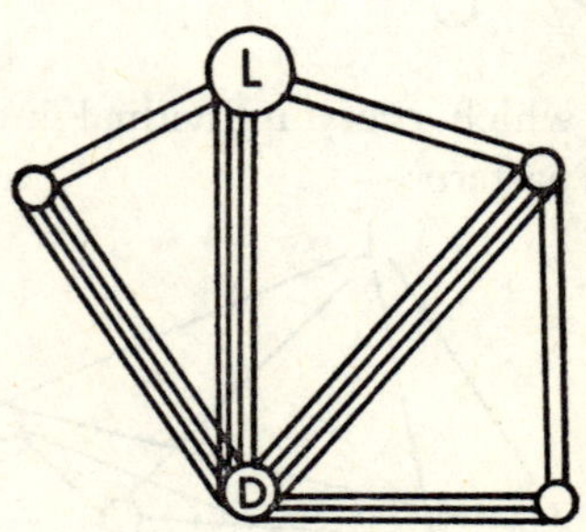

In the last twenty to twenty-five years, interest in working with groups and in studying the effects of group interactions has intensified in psychotherapy, in management training and in education. Nomenclature and practical organisational details vary but the underlying theoretical framework is essentially the same. The use of groups for education in self-awareness is growing, particularly in the training of workers in the personal services.

It was suggested in the first chapter that this growth of interest in human relationship problems has arisen—and could only have arisen—at the point in time when the conquest of the technological and scientific problems makes physical survival easier to achieve. We now have not only greater know-how but a greater measure of affluence, provided by technological advance, which makes the further search for solutions to our human and psychological problems feasible.

In addition it can also be argued that this same technological advance has of itself created pressures on the individual unknown to former generations. Writing of the growth of interest in human relations training, two distinguished members of the School of Management at the Massachusetts Institute of Technology maintain that it is based on 'its singular appropriateness for dealing with some of the core crises facing contemporary society. These crises emerge generally from the acceleration of certain forces often summarised under the word modernisation; that is to say, forces which tend toward increased reliance on science and technology for the solution of man's problems: increased urbanisation, bureaucratisation and mechanisation, particularly of communication systems and higher rates and frequency of mobility, increased population and so forth.

'This tendency toward modernisation makes life problematical for the *individual*. There is already mounting evidence that he is alienated, lonely, anxious, and desperately seeking purpose and identity. It is very difficult to know how far or deep these personal conditions go and what can or should be done to ameliorate them. To make matters worse, the individual is being called upon to perform more and more complicated roles in his world of work. It is no longer enough to be a competent specialist or technician or expert or "entrepreneur". Nowadays, the individual is called on to understand "the human side of enterprise", to develop interpersonal competence, to examine the social and political forces within which his work is embedded and has to be transacted. His success and self-esteem may depend upon these human skills.'[9]

The discussion of 'behaviour in groups' in this chapter will be concerned with what is known about interaction in *small* groups. By 'interaction' is meant exchange of meanings between people—communication in its broadest sense. The most usual method is, of course, talking and listening but often it is done by writing and reading and it also includes gestures and glances and all the non-verbal cues picked up from each other.

A 'small' group is generally considered to have an upward limit of 15 to 20. The use of the word 'group' in this context implies that a number of people are associated together in face to face relations over a period of time and they are mutually aware of each other as members of the same group.

The size is important: a group larger than 20 readily breaks up into sub-groups. The larger the group, the greater the demand on the leader and as the size grows he becomes more and more differentiated from the other members. Gradually he ceases to be just the leading member of the group and tends to become the director of it. A few active members begin to dominate any interchange which takes place and other members cease to participate. A lecturer and an audience are not a group in the sense in which the word is used here.

In a small group seated—symbolically—in a circle it is possible for each member to have eye contact with every other member. Eye signalling, as we have already noted, is a major part of most human interaction: where it is impossible, as with a blind person, some form of physical contact has to be substituted.

In a group of two, i.e. two people interacting, there is likely to be tension and emotion, a high exchange of information and a tendency to avoid disagreement. This tolerance is necessary if the group is to survive (a marriage, for example) because in the absence of a third member there is no outside support for either party. The potential role of children or the couple's parents is of interest in its effect on the marriage bond. Where there are three people a coalition of two to the exclusion of the other is common. In the primary triad of parents and one child a balance has to be maintained if one member is not to feel permanently excluded. Thus maximum satisfaction can only be achieved if the coalitions are constantly shifting. For the marriage to survive the child must at times be excluded, and obliged to seek other contacts and it can very often be observed that the wrath of one parent with the child is balanced automatically by some compensatory action on the part of the other. Children are usually not slow to grasp the potential advantage of being able to pair with either parent in turn and so play one off against the other. The same is true of any other person taken into the intimacy of the household of a married couple.

Groups of even numbers (four, six or eight) produce on average more internal disagreement than odd-numbered groups (three, five or seven) due to the possibility of the formation of sub-groups of equal size. A group of five can be a particularly satisfying size in that the division two: three provides each member with satisfactory support as well as stimulus and it is small enough for personal recognition and participation. A number between four and eight is generally conceded to be the best size for a dinner party: 'more than the Graces and fewer than the Muses'. Above eight it becomes possible for any one individual to withdraw and as the number grows each member has more relationships to maintain and less time to do so.

With large classes—say over twenty—teachers adopt various means to re-arrange the children into smaller sub-groups so that every child can 'relate' to at least a few other members of the class. Otherwise it is possible for a child to avoid contacts and learn very little. Children who are relatively 'uneducated' after several years of school attendance are not unknown. The main argument in favour of using technical devices as an aid to teaching is in order to liberate the teacher for greater personal interaction with each of his pupils.

Small groups of the kind we are considering can be classified in several ways. There are, for example, autonomous groups such as a circle of close friends built on free choice and voluntary association; institutionalised groups like the family; small groups within larger organisations often called mediating groups because they link individuals to the organisation, e.g. small work groups in factories or offices, small groups of friends, mates or buddies among school pupils, college students or soldiers in a division, and problem-solving groups such as committees or teams—in fact any group engaged in a corporate task.

Again one can think of them as task orientated or as mainly concerned with social and emotional satisfactions. Some groups, of course, aim to achieve both objectives such as, for example, voluntary charitable organisations and indeed the most successful work groups are frequently found to be those which incidentally afford social and emotional satisfaction to their members.

All the foregoing statements on the effects of size on group interaction are based on research findings. Among the many other topics which have been explored in detail[10] are:—the effect of introducing new members; the influence of the group on the behaviour of its members and on changing their attitudes and opinions; the social status of members and the conflicts arising when personal goals conflict with group goals. The success of some supportive groups like Alcoholics Anonymous or Weight Watchers or of group work with—say—delinquents is due to the fact that people are more readily influenced as members of a group than as individuals. A sub-group of people with common problems is isolated from the influence of the larger neighbourhood or social group and the individual's motivation towards change is enhanced.

It is important to a member of a group to be clear about the task in hand and discussion to determine aims and method of work is essential. This does not however guarantee that the goals are wholeheartedly endorsed by every member and for many, membership will also be serving other purposes, not necessarily conscious. Thus in the course of their meetings, straightforward rational discussion may at times give way to quixotic outbursts, unexpected voting or some form of special pleading suggesting the existence of a 'hidden agenda' alongside the overt one.

The behaviourist/psychoanalytic controversy over individual therapy seems to have no counterpart among group workers. There is much co-operation and mutual understanding between group psychotherapists and the social scientists and both Foulkes and Bion, for example, make appreciative references to the contribution of the experimentalists towards the interpretation of group interactions.

Among themselves the psychoanalysts have their differences which are of great theoretical interest but there is no firm evidence as yet that in practice these produce significant therapeutic differences. Their differences relate mainly to the early development of the young child. Anna Freud, daughter of the famous father, maintains that children cannot be psychoanalysed until they can talk: Melanie Klein, another famous female analyst, maintains that her analysis of the free-association play of very young children provides firm evidence for her developmental theories.[11] Foulkes, whose work is associated with the Maudsley Hospital, tends to remain closer to Freud and his daughter and emphasises the 'transference' situation in groups, either with the leader or between fellow members. He writes[12]: 'In one group a man and a woman were exchanging information about their respective marital problems and it became clear that a transference relationship existed between them. Each stood for the other's partner in marriage and both were raising questions which each would really have liked to discuss and clarify with his or her spouse. After both had been made conscious of the significance of the situation, neither felt that it would be possible to speak at home as they had in the group. Matters which each found too intimate to discuss with his or her respective husband and wife were not too intimate to discuss with one another in the presence of the group although each was and remained fundamentally a complete stranger to the other as a private person.'

Situations of this kind are very familiar to counsellors running 'free-floating' discussion groups to help young people to explore their intimate feelings and attitudes. For example, both girls and boys will ask questions of an older woman counsellor about intercourse and childbirth, which they would find impossible to discuss with their own mothers.

One important aspect of the transference situation in relation to group work is the role which the group itself can play as an agent for changing attitudes. In the minds of its members it can be felt to represent society as a whole and to set norms for behaviour against which the members assess their own performances. That is, the group takes on a 'culture' of its own. Its standards may be in conflict with those accepted 'outside' the group and be judged by outsiders as either better or worse; a moral improvement as in some pioneering and social reforming groups or as morally corrupting.

Bion, at the Tavistock Institute of Human Relations, has come to regard the work of Melanie Klein as of central importance, particularly her theory of 'projective identification'. This is different from Freud's view of identification which, to quote Bion, was 'almost entirely a process of introjection by the ego'.[13] Others who support (or have supported) Klein's methods and theories are D. W. Winnicott[14] and Susan Isaacs[15] whose educational work with young children at the Malting House School at Cambridge is well known. The psychoanalytic school as a whole tend to take the historical view and to relate the dynamics of group activity in the present to the relationships established in childhood within the primary group of the family. Thus something akin to parental dependence, sexual jealousy or sibling rivalry can be seen to be operating within groups of adults in the here and now. Klein's contribution to the debate is to suggest that the child's response to external objects differs in important ways from that of the adult. The child does not distinguish himself and his own personal feelings from the surrounding world and any object which gives him pleasure becomes to him a 'good object' and one which gives him pain, a 'bad object'. Thus his early emotional life is of an 'all or nothing' kind, peopled either with gods or devils. Indeed it has been suggested that the concepts of heaven and hell are derived from such unconscious memories of early childhood. The child makes no adequate distinction between sensations and their accompanying feelings and impulses nor between those feelings and impulses and the associated outer objects. It is doubtful whether we ever manage a complete distinction between the objective and the subjective since as we have seen, our perception of objects in the outer world is influenced by our attitudes towards them. One of the goals of counselling is to help the person in distress to relate his anger and frustration to feelings within himself rather than view them as an inevitable consequence of some 'bad' external object which as often as not is another person. The young delinquent and the older recidivist share the same defect—their inability to relate their actions to their own inner feelings.

This early impulse to divide the universe into 'good' and 'bad', to project all our painful feelings on to the outer world—the not-self—is only corrected slowly and with difficulty. According to Kleinian theory the qualities projected on to the 'bogies' depend upon the child's stage of development. 'Thus at the earliest or oral stage the projected figures suck, bite, tear or rend; at the anal or urethral levels they are liable to flood the world with filth or water or indulge in other forms of widespread and fierce destructiveness; while at the phallic level they castrate, mutilate and maim—all of these stages finding expression not only in individual childish phantasy but in frequently recurring themes of fairy tale or myth'.[16]

Infantile aggression is projected on to the object—say—the breast—rather than on to a complete person—the mother. He thus endows the mother with his own crude and primitive aggression producing a fierce and barbaric phantasy parent. Psychoanalysts who follow Klein see this as an explanation of the fact which is often observed, that a child's judgements about wrong doing are often harsher and more severe than those of his parents'; in other words his harsh super-ego is introjected not from the parental standards which may be comparatively mild, but from his own aggressive ambivalence towards the good/bad objects which frustrate him. Adolescent members of disciplinary committees are often harsher than their elders.

Thus for the Kleinian School the formation of the super-ego is not a single process connected with a particular psychological stage, but results from a series of introjections over a long period of time each interspersed with a corresponding process of *projection:* an alternating process conducive to personal growth in which the primitive impulses can be gradually replaced by a more realistic super-ego and a more realistic appraisal of the parents and the rest of the outside world. Even so, the early relationships with the family continue to colour our later relationships. The adult in his day to day encounters in social or working groups may be unconsciously searching for a 'father figure' and neurotically concerned with the male object—the penis. Similarly in the search for a mate a man may be unconsciously seeking to replace the mother and her nourishing object—the breast—as well as or even in lieu of, seeking to satisfy his adult sexual needs. Again sibling rivalry for the attention of the parents can be seen as the prototype of the competitiveness of some group activities among adults as well as adolescents.

Members of a group will from time to time identify the leader with various good or bad introjections of their own—a punitive father at one moment or a kindly elder brother at another. Bion, following Klein, maintains that the group can also manipulate the leader, casting him into a role appropriate to the here and now situation and not specifically related to introjections of any one member. The group seems to take on a life of its own ignoring the needs of individuals. Bion quotes examples from his own work in which the group treated him at one moment as a Messiah who would solve all their problems without their having to do any work and at another rejected him as useless.

The group worker interested in the various approaches to therapy is well supplied with cheap texts in which such psychiatric theories can be broadly studied.[17] The most encouraging point for the student to note is that the psychiatric stance is now much less rigid. There is a general recognition of the complexity of the problems and the value not only of the psychoanalytic approach in all its ramifications but also of the contributions of many other types of workers, such as social scientists, social workers, lay counsellors, clergy, anthropologists and linguists.

The symbolism of the unconscious like the symbolism of poetry and myth to which it is clearly akin needs to be read with the eye of the artist not of the scientist. It may not further our knowledge of causes and their effects but cannot fail to enlarge our concept of the human psyche and enable us to accept that every individual is unique. We readily pay lip service to this statement but if we can genuinely accept the creative aspects of mental growth then every encounter—between a counsellor and a new client—will be as it should be, a new voyage of discovery.

The application of group work methods in industry[18] and in educational institutions is already fairly widespread and continues to grow. Argyle[19] provides a short summary of 'T-group' training with some references. Among educational workers from Britain in this field are Mrs Abercrombie,[20] Professor Oeser,[21] A. K. C. Ottaway[22] and Elizabeth Richardson.[23]

Several different names are used to denote this kind of group experience or training which makes for confusion and it is to be hoped that one agreed title will emerge fairly soon. 'T-group' is the one favoured by those concerned with management training and for them the 'T' stands for 'Training'. When used by psychotherapists the 'T' can stand for 'Therapeutic'. 'Laboratory training' usually implying residential courses is another term. The educational workers use 'group work', 'group teaching', and 'group discussion' almost indistinguishably though a good case can be made out (and should be) for distinguishing between 'group discussion' and the title phrase of this chapter 'Group Counselling'. 'Human Relations' training is another name but perhaps the most appropriate for the general overall title which is needed is 'Sensitivity Training'.

In asking for one title for a method which can be used in many differing circumstances I am not overlooking the wide diversity of aims among those who find the method useful. Nor am I suggesting any rigidly agreed pattern in practice. What I do suggest is that although the details and nuances in practice must vary to meet the needs of the practitioners, the similarities are far greater than the differences. Indeed our confidence in the procedure would be undermined if it were not so since the theoretical framework must in every case be based on what firm evidence we get from the psychiatrists and the social scientists about the nature of persons and the nature of groups.

Historically the practice and the research have been pursued simultaneously and this continues to be so. Thus practice must remain flexible and open ended if it is to be responsive to the implications of research findings. This is the justification for suggesting (as this book does by implication) that practitioners in the personal services should be aware of what the theorists are thinking and be acquainted with their research results. Without this open endedness and mutual respect, practice ossifies: the role-script becomes a rigid set piece instead of an informed and intuitive improvisation in response to the contingencies of the situation. To be both informed *and* intuitive means that the facts must not only be known but must have been assimilated and become part of oneself, a process which does not happen overnight.

This is a counsel of perfection and far from easy to achieve. The relationships between practitioners and theorists is often a very uneasy one—the one accusing the other of talking nonsense about situations of which they have no personal experience, the counter-blast being that practitioners work in an *ad hoc* fashion raising 'their own prejudices to the status of a natural law'. Needless to say neither of these extreme accusations is true in general though examples can be found to illustrate each one.

Not all the experiments conducted by research workers have an immediate and obvious relevance to current practice; animal experiments to determine some of the basic principles of learning being a case in point. What is needed is much more communication between the two groups of workers in order to test Homans' major hypothesis once again that 'if interactions between the members of a group are frequent . . . sentiments of liking will grow up between them'.[24] What is certain is that no practitioner in any discipline should forget Lord Kelvin's aphorism in respect of engineers that 'the *practical* man continues to practise the errors of his forefathers'.

The genesis of the use of T-group training in management education can be traced back to meetings—designated 'work-shops'—which began in 1946 sponsored by several bodies including the National Education Association and the Research Center for Group Dynamics of the Massachusetts Institute of Technology.[25] The MIT group was responsible for the research programme, Kurt Lewin being one of the initiators. Unhappily he died early in 1947 at the age of 57.

The aim was the solution of various 'back home' problems

involving the need to change behaviour, and the personnel of the Research Center hoped to be able to test some of their hypotheses about the effects of such conference experiences on the behaviour of the participants. The staff met in the evenings to discuss the day's work and some participants were allowed to listen in to their deliberations. The effect on these ordinary conference members of hearing their own behaviour discussed and analysed was described by observers as 'electric'.[26] As a result subsequent conferences featured a small continuing group at first called the Basic Skills Training (BST) Group in which an observer made records which were later made available to the group for discussion and analysis.

The first two initials were soon dropped and the evolution of T-group training methods has continued from that time, i.e. around 1948, to the present. Among the many problems tackled was the elucidation of the precise function of the T-group in a full programme of training in management. It was realised at an early stage that not all of the aims of management training could be achieved by means of the T-group technique. The central function of such sessions is now agreed to be the examining and analysis of the actual behaviour of the group and its members during the course of their meetings and facts and theories need to be dealt with in separate periods. The problems that can be realistically discussed and solved within the T-group period are *not* the back home managerial problems but those which emerge within the training group itself. The hope is that by concentrating on an analysis of actual on-going behaviour within the existing group, members will internalise (i.e. learn) more effective methods of solving the human problems they are likely to meet on their home ground.

The first 'group relations training laboratory' to be held in Britain was run by visiting Americans and jointly sponsored by the European Productivity Agency and the British Institute of Management,[27] the participants being training officers in British industrial firms. Other British industrialists travelled to the USA for their training. The first two centres of activity to develop in Britain were The Industrial Management Division at the

University of Leeds and The Tavistock Institute of Human Relations. The first staff of the Institute were people who had worked on group rehabilitation for prisoners of war or taken part in the group work involved in the War Office Selection Boards (WOSBs) for Officer candidates. The series of 'leaderless group' tests used by the WOSBs were evolved by W. R. Bion who describes the 'essence of the technique' to be the provision of 'a framework in which selecting officers, including a psychiatrist, could observe a man's capacity for maintaining personal relationships in a situation of strain that tempted him to disregard the interests of his fellows for the sake of his own'.[28] Other well-known names on the first staff list of the Institute were E. L. Trist and Elliott Jaques.

'Group work', 'group teaching', 'group discussion' are terms used in educational institutions to indicate a mode of learning quite distinct from the traditional lecture or class room teaching in which an 'authority' on a subject dispenses the facts to rows of students and pupils. Each 'method' has its place: ignorant discussion cannot replace the learning of facts and the inspirational effect of good teaching or lecturing should not be discounted. However, the growing realisation that learning is not a passive exercise, but that to be effective the learner must be actively involved has stimulated a more experimental approach to teaching/learning methods. If the teacher is to improve his performance he needs to learn from his pupils what has been understood and what are the outstanding gaps. Such feedback also helps the pupil to formulate what he has learned and fit it into the pattern of his own understanding.

Moreover in a group the pupil discovers not only how the teacher sees the subject but how it is seen by each of his peers. Thus they activate each other's learning and encourage exploration and discussion. The realisation that other group members have learning difficulties and may sometimes miss the point makes it less embarrassing to ask questions and admit ignorance.

The improvement of cognitive learning is not, however, the only advantage of the group discussion method nor even perhaps the most important one. To associate the education process only with interaction between the teacher who knows and the pupil who doesn't is a poor preparation for adulthood. In the context of an advanced technological society pupils must learn to regard learning as a process continuing throughout life, not one which finishes at 16, or 18 or 21 or any other definitive age. As they grow older there will not always be an authority on hand to correct their mistakes and keep them right: they will have to read and view for themselves and argue and discuss with their immediate associates. Learning to enjoy learning is at least as important as learning facts and is less likely to happen if all educational time is spent sitting passively in rows. The teacher must be personally involved, be an enthusiast, be warmly disposed to his pupils if they are to be imbued with a desire to know and to understand. To set them material to prepare for themselves and then to participate with them on easy terms within a small active group is a most potent stimulant.

In such groups, particularly among adolescents, discussion rarely remains at the factual, logical level. Differences of opinion soon have an effect on the emotional tone and the group then begins to take on a different function.

Learning about oneself, one's behaviour and one's attitudes is a very special branch of learning and can only happen if there is feedback from associates who are affected by the behaviour and the attitudes. Social and emotional behaviour is learned in the same way as cognitive behaviour is learned, by means of messages of approval or disapproval or indifference at each step of the way. Where there are right and wrong answers the messages are relatively easy to convey, but where the adult world is divided, as it is on social questions and religious and moral issues, the messages the child receives are confused and he is often quite unable to interpret them and we—the adults—are often equally unable to pick up cues from him about his emotional bewilderment. As a means for social education and the exploration of emotional issues discussion in a small circular group is ideal. The arrangement conveys symbolically the notion that there are no experts—the participants, including the adult leader, are fellow explorers. The leader's expertise rests not on any certainty about what attitudes group members should or should not adopt but on a belief in the necessity for the exploratory exercise and in his experience in the handling of controversial issues. He will, of course, have his own well established point of view but to lead such a group successfully he needs to hold his beliefs without bigotry and to be able to tolerate the expression of attitudes with which he himself disagrees.

In most groups of young people formed in schools and colleges and youth clubs one is likely to have many different points of view expressed, but where a group seems to be united on—say—a religious or sexual issue—it then falls to the leader to make sure that the opposing arguments are rehearsed. Only by doing this can he ensure first that the opinions which are held are based on choice between alternatives and not on unthinking acceptance of dogma, and secondly that the timid waverer is given the opportunity to express his doubts.

Misunderstandings about this toleration of expression often referred to as the 'permissive' method arise in two ways:—the equating of the method with a specific philosophy and confusion about the aims of those who use it.

The young learn from the old in a great variety of ways and the method used is a major determinant of the result. An enormous amount of the information we acquire as we grow up is picked up incidentally and it can be accurate or wildly fanciful. Learning by imitation is as good as the model we imitate and learning by didactic methods (grammar, tables or spelling for example) depends upon the level of competence of the teacher. But how do we teach people to be loving, to be 'fair', to be good citizens? If I in fact hate my parents or reject my children what good does it do to tell me I shouldn't? Most people in trouble of this kind are distressed by it. Why? Simply because they know they 'shouldn't'. It used to be thought that when a person said 'I can't help it' he really meant 'I won't. Thanks to the work not only of Freud, but of the behaviourists as well, we now recognise that feelings cannot be generated 'on the say so' but have a long history dependent on past relationships. Our first sexual relationships are formed in the early years within the family. The girl whose father was rejecting and unloving is likely to find it difficult to accept herself as lovable and conversely (to paraphrase Shaw) one of the functions of a mother is to teach her son how to love. Feelings arise from experiences, they cannot be learned from a text book, and the purpose of group discussions on these problems with young people is to enlarge their experiences in these areas. The essential prerequisite is a feeling of 'safety', a feeling of being accepted by the leader of the group as a worthwhile person whose feelings however 'reprehensible' will be respected. Most groups, given time, will endorse this framework and come to accept each other on these terms too and there emerges a group feeling which makes further exploration of their anxieties possible. Such a group is similar in some ways to a therapeutic group but the leader is a counsellor and not a doctor and the members are normal young people not patients, and the relationships are therefore quite different.[29] Group Counselling seems an appropriate term to describe what is going on. The task is to learn something about our emotional nature—our own and other people's—and the leader far from controlling what should or should not be discussed encourages the exploration of feeling, painful as well as joyous, with the avowed aim of encouraging the development of insight and self-knowledge.

E. J. Anthony wrote the introductory chapter (among others) of the Foulkes and Anthony book on 'Group Psychotherapy'[30] already referred to. In it he talks of the dichotomy between our inner and outer standards of behaviour as follows. 'In illuminating contrast to life in primitive communities, people reared in the Western civilised world appear to have a good deal to hide. There is a striking prevalence of shame, embarrassment, and other socially unhealthy attitudes. Submerged though he is in his environment, the individual more often than not finds himself unable to express his spontaneous views on a large number of topics that affect him deeply but are tabooed for normal intercourse. Some revelations may break through in confessionals, revivalist meetings, or diaries, but for the great majority opportunity is rarely provided for the unlocking of the innermost chambers of personal feeling. For them, private and public living is kept apart, and socially-acceptable attitudes are put on with their clothes, being taken off only under conditions of emotional security or intoxication. So automatic may this arrangement become in time that the two aspects of personality merge harmoniously into each other, and the act of disavowal is lost in the endless routine of the day.'

He goes on to say that this split between our wishful thinking and our need to conform socially is responsible for much of our anxiety and guilt and this in turn is reflected in the emphasis placed on 'confessional secrecy' between patients and doctors, counsellors and clients. The breaking of this 'inviolate privacy' by the advent of group methods he sees as a great advance in therapeutic practice.

It would be of course absurd to imagine that group work of a purely verbal kind is the miracle technique which will solve all our educational problems in this area. Communication is not linked only to the spoken word and teachers and practitioners of art and drama are experimenting in a variety of ways. Many repertory theatre companies, for example, see themselves as having an educational role to play in the local community and encourage young people to participate in drama groups in which they improvise and act out here and now situations in any way they choose. This often proves a most potent instrument for the exploration of their own feelings. The consequent release of tension and the freeing of the individual for further explorations is a form of counselling in groups which may prove to be the method of choice for a large number of young people including perhaps those with limited verbal skills.

REFERENCES

1. Foulkes, S. H., '*On Group Analysis*', International Journal Psychoanalysis, 1946, **27**, 5.
2. Bion, W. R. and Rickman, J., '*Intra-Group Tensions in Therapy*', Lancet, Nov. 27th, 1943. Reprinted in *Experiences in Groups and Other Papers*', W. R. Bion, Tavistock, 1961. (Social Science Paperback 1968).
3. Klein, Josephine, *The Study of Groups*, Routledge Paperback, ed. 1967, p. 106.

4. *Ibid*, p. 175
5. 'Gestalt' is a German word which is untranslatable. The nearest the English language can get is 'configuration'.
6. Köhler's work is discussed on pp. 37–38.
7. See Vernon, M. D., *Perception*, Penguin Books, 1962.
8. Lewin K. '*Principles of Topological Psychology*', trans. F. Heider and G. M. Heider, N.Y., McGraw-Hill, 1936, and '*Field Theory and Learning*', Ch. 4 in *The Psychology of Learning*, Nat. Soc. Stud. Educ. 41st Yearbook Part II, pp 215–242, N.Y., McGraw-Hill, 1936.
9. Schein, Edgar H. and Bennis, Warren G., *Personal and Organizational Change through Group Methods*, John Wiley & Sons, N.Y., 1965, p. 6.
10. See Klein, Josephine, *op. cit.*
11. Klein, Melanie, *The Psychoanalysis of Children*, Hogarth Press, 1932.
12. Foulkes, S. H. and Anthony, E. J., *Group Psychotherapy*, Penguin Books, new edition 1965, pp. 219–230.
13. *Ibid*, Tavistock, 1961, Final Section on Group Dynamics, p. 141.
14. Isaacs, Susan, *Intellectual Growth in Young Children*, Routledge & Kegan Paul.
15. Winnicott, D. W., *Collected Papers*, London, Tavistock, 1958.
16. Flügel, J. C., *Man, Morals and Society*, Duckworth, 1945, p. 112.
17. e.g. Brown, J. A. C., *Freud and the Post-Freudians*, Penguin Books, 1961.
18. The Glacier Metal Project is perhaps the best known in Britain. See Jaques, Elliott, *The Changing Culture of a Factory*, Tavistock, 1951.
19. Argyle, Michael, *ibid*, pp. 193–196.
20. Abercrombie, M. L. Johnson *The Anatomy of Judgement* Penguin Books, 1969. Also *Aims and Techniques of Group Teaching*. Monograph of the Society for Research in Higher Education, 1970.
21. Oeser, O. A., *Teacher, Pupil and Task*, Tavistock, 1955. (Now Professor of Psychology, University of Melbourne.)

22. Ottaway, A. K. C., *Learning through Group Experience*, Routledge & Kegan Paul, 1965.
23. Richardson, Elizabeth, *Group Study for Teachers*, Routledge Paperback, 1967.
24. Homans, G. C., *The Human Group*, Routledge & Kegan Paul, London, 1950, p. 112.
25. Out of the initial association of these two groups grew the National Training Laboratories (NTL) a body responsible for the enormous development of this kind of training in the field of Industrial Management in the USA
26. Lippitt, Ronald, *Training in Community Relations*, N.Y., Harper Bros., 1949, gives a detailed account of these early training programmes and the research results.
27. British Institute of Management: Report on E.P.A. project No. 399 on Group Dynamics, 1956.
28. Bion, W. R., *The Leaderless Group Project*, Bull. Menninger Clinic 10, 77–81, 1946.
29. Cf. Ch. 1, p. 6.
30. Foulkes, S. H. and Anthony, E. J., *Group Psychotherapy*, Penguin Books, 1957 edition.

Chapter 4

Selection and Training for Counselling

Discussions on appropriate selection and training procedures for any job need to begin with a job analysis. What are we selecting and training for? What skills does a counsellor use? With this question answered the next two follow: how do you select people with the potential to develop these skills and what sort of a training programme will actually ensure their development.

Two aspects of the counselling job have been discussed in the previous two chapters. It can be done individually or in groups. It can be described as an encounter between one person—the incumbent—and either one other person under some emotional stress or a group of people who share a common emotional problem. The aim is to help the person (whether alone or in a group) to a greater awareness of the nature of his difficulties so that he is able to find an acceptable way to resolve them. The method used in the attempt to achieve this objective is to offer him a relationship with a person—a counsellor—not emotionally involved in his difficulties—a relationship which is bounded by a structure which should be well defined and understood by both parties. The quality of this relationship and its effectiveness in achieving the aim of counselling will clearly depend on the nature of the counsellor. The first essential is an ability to establish rapport and produce a relaxed atmosphere in which the client feels safe enough to talk. The behavioural skills involved in this have already been mentioned.[1] Secondly the counsellor must be alert and percipient, able to pick up clues from the behaviour of his client—his tone of voice—hesitations—intermittent nervousness—the ideas he dodges—likely to provide some insight into his condition which he is unaware of or at least unable to convey verbally. To reflect back these impressions in such a way that the client is free to accept or deny them requires the counsellor to be very sensitive to the impression he himself is having on the person in front of him.

The role of the counsellor in a so-called 'non-directive' encounter is often thought to be a totally passive one but listening and observing acutely in the manner just described involves the whole person. Furthermore, choices have to be made from among all the many impressions flowing in from the client about which area in this person's life it might be most profitable to explore. The throw away line, the sudden switch from one topic or person to another might be indicative of painful areas about which he is ambivalent—on the one hand needing to discuss them and on the other hoping to dodge them. It is not impossible that these are the very areas most closely related to his difficulties.

There is always a temptation to talk about 'the problem', about the persons involved and who did this or said that—concrete issues which are relatively safe—and to deny the existence of any deeper involvement. The experienced person knows that whether or not a client is 'telling the truth' is not necessarily of great importance. The details, the specific facts are often of no great significance. What is important is to concentrate on the individual to discover the emotional impact of the situation—what it *feels* like—for the person concerned.

A man who was anxious to keep his marriage intact and at the same time preserve his relationship with another woman strenuously denied many times to his counsellor that the relationship with the second woman was a sexual one. When the counsellor discovered that he had been deceived he was very angry and unwilling to try to help him. 'I'm a very tolerant man, I can take the drunkard, the violent, the homosexual, the transvestite, but what I will not stand is lying. Clients must not lie to me.' His tolerance had its limits which, of course, limited his ability to help. This applies to all of us but with training and experience the limits of what we are able to tolerate from clients can be extended.

Counsellors need to be competent to discuss in a broad general way what makes a man what he is. What motivates him; what are his ideas of morality and religion—questions related to his system of values. This sometimes means listening to views which run counter to our own and our tolerance may again evaporate so that we find ourselves arguing a case. Meanwhile the client's 'problem' remains unresolved.

Most of the dilemmas which people bring to a counsellor do not have one 'correct' solution. The trials and tribulations of life are tackled in different ways by different people depending upon circumstances, character, personality, value systems and many other factors. A wage of £30 a week is to one man highly satisfactory and to another penury. One disabled person will rejoice that his condition is no worse: another make his life miserable with complaints. With clients as with counsellors, behaviour, such as for example physical aggression, will be tolerated by one person and abhorred by another. It is frequently an important part of counselling to help the person to sort out his own particular hierarchy of values—what things are of special importance to him and what of less: what circumstances he finds intolerable and which ones he can ride easily. A man's or a woman's hopes are often locked in the heart, unexpressed but nevertheless motivating behaviour in ways which may seem incomprehensible. An apparently trivial quarrel may be sparked off because the immediately trivial object is related to some unspoken fear. A couple who came for help reported that they were always quarrelling and couldn't understand what had happened because they were still very much in love. The immediate quarrel was about the location of an electric point. Unless we are ready to accept that when a person says he's worried he has something worth worrying about, we might in this instance be tempted to dismiss such a quarrel as mere childishness. As these two talked, separately, the woman's deep fear and the man's unspoken frustration became evident to themselves. This was a marriage between two people of humble social origin. The husband was studying and felt himself to be changing his status to that of a professional middle-class person. The words are mine not his: he had never allowed his feelings and ambitions to become explicit because he sensed the threat to his wife. She felt safe living near her family and continuing to live as they did but had an unexpressed fear that her husband was going to change it all. She was too fond of him and too loyal and too afraid that she would prove inadequate to risk facing this major issue. Any semblance of change in their pattern of living, like using the dining room to eat in occasionally instead of the kitchen, raised sparks from this hidden volcano. A common enough problem and one they were later able to laugh about but in the early days a potential source of bitterness and regret.

In this case the bond was a strong one and when faced with an imaginary choice between the cosiness of her family and her husband's needs she had no doubts. It is often helpful to consider the question 'In the last resort which would you choose—what would you do—where would you go?' To consider, in fact, the ultimate goal around which a person's life is built. Counsellors, as persons, have their own hierarchy, their own goals for themselves. However important to them their own moral and religious beliefs, their own hierarchy of values, they must be able to see them as personal possessions not to be confused with the personal value systems of their clients. There is of course a place for proselytising, for preaching and for persuading but it is not in the counselling room. Any book with a message, which includes this one, is written to persuade people to a point of view but when a person's emotional life is in confusion and he acts in ways he doesn't wish to act and hates when he would prefer to love, telling him what he ought to do is worse than useless. A person cannot change his attitudes because someone tells him to do so but only if the change is in harmony with his own inner needs.

Over great areas of life the brain and the body function together without conscious awareness: it is when needs conflict that we become aware and uneasy. If the solution that is 'right' for the individual is to be found he must be totally involved in discovering it.

It is easy to pay lip service to the idea of accepting people as they are until we meet someone whose condition arouses our disapproval. It is sentimental to pretend that we love all our fellow men. It is, I imagine, practically impossible to do so. I know I cannot manage it. Accepting them as worthy of help, even though we may deplore their actions is another matter and requires a measure of objectivity and tenacity, a willingness to look the facts in the face. Man's inhumanity to man is often hard to bear and to be able to bear it requires resilience and optimism. On the whole, social work is not for the squeamish.

Finally, and prosaically, a counsellor needs to be reasonably well informed about the various stages of human development; able to recognise signs of mental breakdown or physical illness; alive to legal difficulties and knowledgeable about where further advice on such matters can readily be obtained.

With the foregoing analysis in mind we can now sum up the requirements for the job. First and most important: skill in human relationships which includes behaviour which is friendly, warm and outgoing, ignoring social barriers; an ability to listen and a percipient sensitivity to the behaviour of others. Without this primary ability counselling cannot begin. Secondly: a recognition of the complexity of human motivation and the diversity of possible goals; an acceptance of ambivalence and unconscious drives; a realisation that although man is capable of change, his present condition is what it is largely on account of past experience. In short, tolerance and reluctance to apportion blame. Third: a tough streak and absence of sentimentality. Fourth: moderate intelligence; some education and a grip on the practicalities.

It will be appreciated that this is not an assignment for sentimental do-gooders, nor a job prescription for 'middle-class people with time on their hands who like telling working class people how to live'.

SELECTION

Having described the job, we now turn to the problem of selecting persons potentially capable of doing it. The easy items are at the end. Selection of people with a moderate level of intelligence and education can be achieved by screening out those who do very badly on an intelligence test and those whose education has been minimal. In voluntary work most candidates are self-selected on these vectors and the intelligence testing and the biographical forms are often largely a formality. They are however an essential safeguard: a few may have to be turned away on these grounds. With full-time students on social work courses entry standards are designed to take care of intellectual level but in choosing mature students for social work courses this part of the selection procedure is very important. Examination results are no doubt limited in value but they do at least indicate a modicum of intelligence and ability to learn. Without them other tests of competence have to be substituted.

The other criteria relate mainly to aspects of the candidate's personality and to his attitudes. Many objective procedures are available for the assessment of these—mostly of the self-rating kind—but, as with most psychological testing, their use in predicting subsequent behaviour is based on a statistical exercise. For example, we may be able to say that out of ten people with a score of x on Test A, seven are likely to do well on Task B but what the statisticians cannot tell us is who are the three individuals who will not succeed. So the selection on personality grounds must be a sequential process involving what have been called by Cronbach and Gleser of Illinois, narrow band and wide band procedures.[2] These authors discussing the importance of Decision Theory conclude 'Nothing in our argument leads us to think that any procedure can conceivably give an accurate analysis of the "whole personality". Instead it is necessary to distil from a limited quantity of information the most intelligent possible decision. The problem is to find the procedure which, in the time available, offers the greatest yield of important, relevant, and interpretable information'.

The first major project in this country for the selection of candidates on personality grounds was made during the Second World War by the War Office Selection Boards (WOSBs) and the Civil Service Selection Boards (CSSBs) and so-called 'Cissbe' and 'Wosbe' procedures are now fairly widely recognised.[3] They involve observations and ratings of behaviour in a variety of circumstances by a group of selectors. Accepting that an individual's judgement of another person is biased in ways related to the selector's own personality, the pooled opinions of four or five judges are considered to be better than that of one person making a judgement on his own since their various prejudices are likely to cancel each other out. In their book on 'Personnel Selection in the British Forces' Vernon and Parry state in their conclusions that: 'War Office Selection Boards have shown the superiority of thorough study of candidates by several trained judges to ordinary interview methods of selection and this aspect of WOSB procedure is worth applying to the selection of managers, administrative civil servants and in other high grade occupations.'[4]

This method of pooling subjective judgements can be used for various purposes. The marking of English essays, for example, is notoriously unreliable but it has been shown that if an essay is set in an entrance examination the averaged results of four markers making quick subjective judgements predict future success in English better than the marks of any one judge taken separately.[5] Presumably the marker who penalises bad spelling is cancelled out by the chap whose pet hate is poor handwriting: the method accepts that bias is inevitable and makes allowances for it.

Care must be taken that no judge has access to the marks given by another. When using several selectors to make judgements about personality they will vary among themselves over which aspects of behaviour they regard as important and it is essential that their ratings be made quite independently. Cronbach and Gleser insist that judges must be trained: that is they must be aware of the pitfalls. We are all suggestible and a knowledge of the opinion of a fellow judge cannot fail to influence our own. It we suspect his opinion the influence will be in one direction and if we respect it, it will be in another. Any comparing of notes or discussion of candidates or even exchange of gestures defeats the purpose: four judgements are only better than one if they are made totally independently.

Two other hazards are the 'halo' effect and the 'tendency to the mean'. Personality has many facets and a judge may be called upon to make several separate ratings about each individual. He must therefore fully accept the fact that in his first meeting with the candidate he will tend to make a quick appraisal which will be either negative or positive. Unless he observes actual *behaviour* in the various situations and where possible records objectively what is done or said, each rating is likely to be coloured by the first impression. Good looks, a friendly smile, an intelligent remark will have a 'halo' effect on ratings of other qualities—such as consistency, sticking power, tolerance, which are quite unrelated. The influence of an unfavourable impression has been referred to as 'horn' effect!

'The tendency to the mean' is a statistician's phrase which I am using here to refer to the reluctance to use extreme ratings. In assessing behaviour it is difficult to make use of more than five categories such as for example:—very good; good; average; poor; very poor. For some procedures three will do:—Yes; not certain; no; for others two:—in; out. The experienced selector makes effective use of all the categories he is given in order the better to distinguish one candidate from the next. The method of paired comparisons is a useful device for deciding an order of merit: do I rank Mr A above Miss C or below? If forced to choose would I have Mrs X or Mr Y? and so on throughout the list.

Whatever selection procedure is adopted should be subject to validation. In selecting for counselling and social casework this is not difficult since in-service assessment or supervision is essential for good work and it is possible to compare grades at selection with subsequent gradings on the job. If this is to be of maximum value all the categories should be used whenever possible. To rate everyone 'average' and reserve the 'very good' category in case the archangel Gabriel turns up one day, is useless. Difficulties arise when people are selected in small groups on numerous occasions over a period of time as they are, for example, in selecting counsellors or case workers or potential army officers or in marking annual examination papers. A proper statistical use of a five-point scale would mean that over a period the total intake would consist of about 10% very good (A) ratings and 10% very poor (E), 20% good (B) and 20% poor (D) and 40% (C) in the average category. In other words the definition of 'very good' in any situation should be related to the likely calibre of the top ten per cent of the total potential intake, *not* to some subjective and abstract idea of excellence.

This is of course difficult if not impossible to determine *a priori* and has to be settled from experience over a period of time or at the outset by comparison with other well-established agencies. Judges must arrive at some such agreement because sub-groups will vary in quality and if the correct statistical spread were to be applied meticulously in each small selection unit the 'A' candidates in a 'poor' group would not be the equal of 'A' candidates in a 'good' group and there would be an in-built failure rate of 10% regardless of the quality of the lowest tenth of the candidates in each separate batch. However hard they work to objectify their ratings judges are unlikely to avoid this difficulty entirely. It is not unknown in university departments when first and second class honours categories are being decided and assessing personality variables is notoriously more unreliable than marking examination papers. A balance has to be struck between fair play for candidates and fair play for clients.

It remains to discuss what aspects of the candidate the judges should be asked to rate. Ideally these should be closely linked to the job analysis and in the case of counselling would include: ability to accept people and listen to what they say: sensitivity to non-verbal and other cues in face to face encounters: tolerance of differences of opinion or of values together with freedom from prejudice. They should not be asked to *rate* intelligence as this is much better done by the objective test but positive indications of intelligent behaviour in relation to the job in hand, quick wittedness, easy grasp of essentials are clearly important and should not pass unnoticed. In some cases, and these mainly among older candidates, such observations may run counter to the test result and with borderline scores they may add or detract.

Thus, the task of the selector is to place candidates in as many differing situations as is possible in the time available, so that various items of his behaviour can be monitored.

The residential selection initiated by the WOSBs has many advantages. Tension among candidates is unavoidable but is more quickly reduced in a residential setting where there is opportunity for everyone to meet socially. Few of us are capable of worrying very much about our 'image' at breakfast time. From the selector's point of view this is pure gain. The old crack among officer recruits that 'they' needed to see whether you ate your peas with a knife has the spirit of truth. Learning how to get selected—learning the 'right' answers to questionnaires—is quite naturally a game that any intelligent candidate tries to play, a ploy that was guyed very amusingly by W. H. Whyte.[6] However, selectors need to get a glimpse of the person behind the actor and they do not expect a candidate to be white all through.

The relaxation we achieve around the dinner table is often in delightful contrast to that which we are unable to avoid at breakfast. I remember, many years ago (before the Arab-Israeli question had become so explosive) overhearing a conversation at the other end of my table around which there were seven candidates and myself. A young and charming woman, all sweetness and light during the discussion sessions, was holding forth about Zionism. She had, it transpired, been born in the Middle East and was completely pro-Arab. My neighbour happened to be a quiet self-effacing Jewess and I whispered to her 'Aren't you going to join in?' She replied 'Not at any price—please keep me out of it'. I, of course, had no intention of drawing attention to my presence. Suddenly our Arab lady stopped talking and there was a somewhat embarrassed silence until she said 'Good heavens, what have I done? When I left home yesterday my husband kissed me goodbye and said "Have a good time, dear, and remember *DON'T* mention the Arabs"'. The release of tension at our table was heard all over the dining room. In case readers are curious to know the end of the story I perhaps ought to add that the lady was accepted !

The main problem of residential selection is the economic one and in most selection situations non-residential meetings have to suffice. They should however be planned by the day, not the hour, and thus include as many as possible of the group activities that would be included in a residential selection conference.

The procedures should be chosen to mirror the on-the-job situation as far as possible. For counsellors and caseworkers the following three would be obligatory:—case discussion sessions in which actual cases are presented similar to those which are likely to be met in practice: leaderless discussions on controversial topics in which qualities of leadership, aggression, tolerance—and so on—quickly display themselves; and individual interviews in which the selectors can seek whatever personal information they deem relevant to the particular job.

There are numerous other ways in which the attitudes of candidates can be examined, some of which will be mentioned here and others dealt with later in the section on training.

Case discussion

Actual cases are usually presented verbally or on paper and may deal with—students, young workers, married couples, engaged people, divorcees, destitute families, people on probation—whichever type of client is appropriate. Newcomers to such work will have their own immediate naïve reaction to the problems raised and in rare cases may decide the job is not for them. A common reaction is to regard the problems presented as trivial, readily capable of solution with a little rationality and/or compromise. 'If she doesn't want to go to Devon and he doesn't want to stay in London what about a house in the Cotswolds'. In this particular case the man had just retired from the services and was feeling that his 'home' was not *his* home but a common reaction to the story is that 'he is being unreasonable' and 'will soon get over it'. It is important to discover how far a candidate is able to 'feel' the overriding importance of feeling and accept the irrelevance of a 'commonsense' approach to human relationships. Case discussions are of course the main basis of in-service training and their use in selection presents a difficulty. Candidates become interested and involved and tempt the selector to embark on a training course. The interest and involvement is of great value: it allows the candidates to learn more about the job and the selectors to learn more about the candidates but to spill over into training is a waste of valuable time at this juncture. Nevertheless candidates often feel very frustrated by being allowed only a momentary glimpse of what the job is like.

I know no selector who would want to dispense entirely with the discussion of case material during a selection programme but the use of it pinpoints one of the major problems of selection in this field. That is, how far the qualities needed for counselling are inborn and how far they can be developed by training. As was indicated in Chapter 2 many people who see themselves as potential counsellors have a fairly clear view of how they think people should behave and by and large the rest of us feel that they are the last people to be allowed to engage in this work. It is arguable that they differ from those who are selected for counselling only in degree. They declare consciously and overtly where they stand while counsellors agree that they themselves have unconscious wishes to control people which they must struggle to become aware of in order to improve their work. All of us who have experience of casework or counselling recognise that we have learnt a great deal from our clients as well as from the training. Probably some of the people we reject could also learn even if it were to take a little longer.

Self-selection for a job implies reasonable motivation to learn so if we take the learning theorists seriously as I am sure we should, a refusal to teach needs some justification. One reason (and another more important one is discussed later, pp. 107–109) is on the grounds of expediency—that unless candidates have already developed some degree of insight into human motivation, including their own, a longer and therefore more expensive period of training would be necessary. The point is plausible but unproven.

Most counsellors, caseworkers and therapists remember their first clients or patients very well: the reasons are obvious. My own first case is, I think, relevant to this discussion: it has the merit of being amusing rather than sad and is of such ancient vintage that my ego is no longer involved. It concerned a rather odd little lady who looked at least 50 but was in fact much younger. She had dabbled in a number of the less orthodox religious sects such as Spiritualists and Four Square Gospellers. Her husband was a working man with a small wage whose behaviour according to her was 'not exemplary' and therefore she would not at first allow me to approach him. She had one son who was a pupil at a private school. No other school would do and she earned the fees by doing various sewing and domestic jobs.

She treated me as a gentlewoman who needed protection from the more disagreeable facts of life. As far as I was eventually able to discover, the reason she was reluctant to let me meet her husband was that he occasionally swore and liked a pint of beer.

Her 'presenting problem' as we say in the jargon was a straightforward one which I lost sight of by the second interview and I had to be reminded of it by her husband two months later. Barbara Wootten who wrote that devastating chapter on social workers[7] could have had a great deal of fun at my expense. Mrs X brought with her a cousin and her illegitimate baby whom, out of compassion, she had housed for some months before and after the child's birth. Now her husband had insisted that the young woman and her child leave their house and Mrs X's problem was 'should she go with her?' Our meetings went on for eight to ten weeks, always on a Friday afternoon, when my client invariably arrived with her small case packed for a weekend visit to some relative or other who was 'in trouble and needing' her. Conscientiously I concentrated our discussions on the state of her marriage—to what extent her husband needed her or she him. Leaving him in favour of one or other of her many relatives was no sudden whim, it had gone on all her married life. The moment she was pregnant she had gone back to Mother and stayed there on and off until the child was several months old. Aunt Fanny had only to sneeze for her to take off and nurse her for a weekend. Seen in retrospect my efforts to get her to see that this was no way for a wife to behave were hilarious and—fortunately—totally unsuccessful. Why she clung to me I don't know: I guess the visits were seen as a pleasant social encounter with an innocent and kind lady who perhaps—could it be—looked as if she 'needed help'. Finally I was allowed to invite her husband to see me. He came, cloth-capped and deferential, and sat down within touching distance.

Me: 'Your wife clearly hasn't been much of a wife to you all these years.'

He—incredulous: '*How* do *you* know that?'

Me: 'Well . . . I've been seeing her for a long time now . . . it would be very surprising . . . '

He—patting me gently on the knee: 'But we'll not change her now, will we?'

I learned a great deal from this episode and it is pretty clear that I needed to learn. Because of my teetotal upbringing I was convinced that I would be no good with marriages which were the worse for drink but the first drinking husband I encountered disproved that theory in no time at all. What I was quite unaware of, with my self-image of a modern wife and mother with a professional job, was that I was about as modern as Eve. My inbuilt concept of the wife's role would have done justice to my grandmother—her duty was to minister to her husband and cook his Sunday dinner and here I had in front of me a woman professing to be religious and compassionate who consistently left her husband to cook for himself and was quite unable to see anything wrong with it.

I heard the relief in her husband's voice over 'our' inability to change her: *he* wasn't trying and had *I* been successful their union would really have been ruined. He had settled for the kind of wife he had, many many years previously and enjoyed his freedom to go to the pub when he liked and 'preferred' his own cooking. So what was it all about? He told me. 'Do something for me'. he said. 'When you next see her, tell her—she won't accept it from me—that she can go to her relatives as often as she likes but I will *not* have any of them in my house. It's too small and I like my own chair by the fire. The baby must *not* come back—I can't stand baby's washing in my sitting room. And *if* she decides to go too that's all right with me but—mark this and tell her I mean it—if she once goes the door will be locked. She will not come back'. I told her and she decided to stay.

Leaderless discussions[8]

In contrast to a case discussion led by one of the selectors the candidates can be seated in a circle without a leader and asked to discuss some controversial topic. The selector sits inconspicuously outside the circle to listen and record. Any topic likely to provoke argument will do: corporal punishment—the death penalty—'permissiveness'—abortion—youth—money.

The selector needs to have experience of working with small groups and thus be able to observe perceptively the role which each candidate plays and how he relates to the other members. This can be expected to vary from one topic to another but the situation provides ample opportunity for observation of attitudes and in particular, tolerance of other people's opinions.

Religious belief is one of the most controversial of topics and is therefore usually avoided in 'polite' society, but in free floating discussions of this kind it rears its head not infrequently. Christian beliefs are cited as a reason for not agreeing to—shall we say divorce or abortion or contraception or whatever—and battle may be joined. I well remember one candidate who called herself an atheist, saying incredulously to a bishop's wife, 'But you don't believe all that guff, do you?' What conclusions should one draw? Does this rate an E? Or conversely what about the lay preacher who says he would not want to counsel an adulterer because it would be condoning his sin. He believed that the only thing to do was to tell him to stop and go back to his wife.

Interviewing

Candidates may be expected to have separate individual interviews with one, two or three selectors one of whom may be a psychiatrist. If there is to be more than one the judges should agree between them what ground each will cover so that the candidate is spared the tedium of answering the same questions for different interviewers.

The interview should be carefully planned and used as an additional test for the collection of data about the candidate: the time should not be wasted collecting information which can be more quickly and accurately assembled by means of questionnaires and objective tests. If it is badly conducted the level of prediction obtainable by means of examination and test results together with biographical data may actually be *decreased* by the addition of an interview rating.

There are several methods of obtaining information from a candidate's verbal reports which differ according to the degree of control over the situation exerted by the interviewer or by the candidate. In formal questionnaires with written responses or tightly structured interviews where the responses are by word of mouth, the investigator has complete control over the questions to be answered. In semi-structured interviews the topics are predetermined but the questions are open-ended e.g.—'What do you think about votes at eighteen?' The unstructured interview gives the candidate even more freedom of response: the topic is only loosely defined and the candidate allowed to respond in his own way. It allows the interviewer to assess the candidate's attitudes and to record the emotional tone of his communications. Because of the breadth and depth of the potential responses such interviews are sometimes labelled 'depth' interviews. This terminology has nothing to do with the degree of consciousness of the attitudes assessed and should not be confused with the use of the word 'depth' in psychoanalytic literature.

At the extreme of this range of procedures is the psychiatric interview in which, typically, there is no set topic and the candidate is encouraged to talk freely about himself. The 'free association' of the psychoanalytic couch is the ultimate in freedom of choice where not only are there no external constraints but the subject himself is expected to exert no conscious control over what he is saying.

The first requirement in any interview is to establish rapport and in an assessment interview the interviewer's first concern must be to produce a relatively relaxed atmosphere in order to reduce the candidate's anxiety. At least thirty minutes should be allocated to each candidate and the first few minutes are usually taken up with small talk and social chat to establish an 'equal-status' relationship, usually symbolised by the absence of a table and a face to face arrangement of two comfortable chairs: the more anxious the candidate the longer the introductory exchange.

The interview itself should be of the 'unstructured' type which does not mean 'unplanned'. Topics should be allocated to each interviewer, but the questions should be open-ended and discussion related to the biographical and other data which the interviewer should have in front of him. Most of the information favourable to the candidate will have been supplied so the interview provides an opportunity to explore neglected areas and adverse information. Part of the skill of interviewing lies in the ability to do this without appearing to be too threatening: face-saving is essential and the interview should end in a friendly manner.

The topics to be covered will be determined by the nature of the work the candidate hopes to do: among counsellors and social workers the motivation which prompted him towards—problem families, probation, marital work—may well be questioned and some assessment of his emotional stability or the stability of his intimate relationships may be felt to be necessary.

In a recent account[9] of residential courses for postgraduate social workers Douglas Woodhouse, Director of the Family Discussion Bureau (now the Institute of Marital Studies) considers the problems of social workers in relation to the kinds of work they opt to do and in particular the emotional impact on them of intensive study of marital relationships. 'It has become clear from the Bureau's various training commitments that profound unconscious forces are touched upon when marital relationships are the central theme of teaching.' The reluctance of many caseworkers, including those with considerable experience, to see and pay attention to the interaction between married partners in their work was discussed at a conference held in 1960.[10] Whatever work they do, workers need to examine themselves and their own difficulties but 'it is our experience' says Dr Woodhouse that marital work 'intensifies' this need and special training is necessary if they are to use the marriage relationship as a focus for casework with family problems (i.e. not only in marital work *per se*). This reluctance to 'work with the marriage' in spite of a growing acceptance of the need to do so requires explanation.

'Probably the most important aspect of this problem has to do with the worker's ability to retain his own identity and a core of assurance that he is not lost in the morass of the other's, the client's, distress . . . At one level, in casework at least, the setting itself tends to support the worker in his capacity to differentiate himself from the client and it may be assumed that the ability of the setting to sharpen the differentiation plays a part in the self-selection by caseworkers of one field rather than another in which to pursue their careers in social work. It is possible to discern a double movement here. The Probation Officer or the Psychiatric Social Worker employed in mental hospitals, for example, may be drawn towards manifestations of delinquency or of madness in their clients which represent, by means of projective identification, their own 'delinquent', their own 'madman'. Such choice can be seen as an attempt by the workers to re-establish contact with a split-off part of themselves. But the demarcation line between the overt delinquent and the Probation Officer, and between the in-patient and the PSW are underlined sufficiently by the palpable limits set by the setting which afford workers some tangible reassurance that real differences do exist between themselves and their clients. (It is the delinquent who has been before the Court: it is the patient who has to stay in hospital). Thus, the double task of offering help to the client, and of gaining 'self-help' for the worker can proceed without too much anxiety, and with profit to both.

'Once into the field of marital difficulties (which confront all caseworkers and most often in disguised ways) the line of demarcation is liable to become so blurred, and at times so indistinguishable, as to be gravely threatening. Even in the Bureau itself, which is a highly supportive setting in this regard, we are always conscious of a persistent tendency to work with the illness or difficulty of each partner and that this is often a defence against awareness of the *interaction* between them. Unlike overt delinquency or psychosis, disorders from which some degree of separateness can be maintained, marriage is inescapably alive in everyone, whether they are married or single. The marriage of our parents and our ambivalence about this relationship, which we both want to split and to repair, continues to exert its powerful influence on our behaviour and relationships. To meet clients' marital problems at depth involves risking the loss of separateness; for the majority of caseworkers, the setting is of relatively little support in the situation. We have come to recognise this as an important factor contributing to the reluctance of trainees (whether they be caseworkers or members of the allied professional groups, e.g. doctors or clergy) to involve themselves in marital problems and in the difficulty encountered in recognising them when they are present in symptoms other than overt marital stress.

'When training relentlessly centres on the interaction between husband and wife and seeks to promote understanding of the links between patterns of early childhood relationships and their later restatement in the heterosexual relationships of marriage, infantile feelings, anxieties and resistance are inevitably stirred up. This is particularly so in as much as psychosexual problems are seldom, if ever, absent in marital work. But just as marriage affords an opportunity for growth and maturation and, at the same time, a field in which there can be a repetition of the central aspects of past experience, with their inherent regressive elements, so, in learning which aims to add knowledge of marital interaction to a worker's professional equipment, processes of growth and regression will go side by side.'[11]

In the selection and training of voluntary workers for marital counselling as is done by the National Marriage Guidance Council and the Catholic Marriage Advisory Council such considerations are of paramount importance and are the justification for a screening interview with a psychiatrist and stringent standards of selection. The arguments also provide strong support for the notion of a specialised agency concentrating mainly on marital work.

Standardised tests

The examination of behaviour and social interaction by clinical methods such as discussion in groups or individual interviews is imprecise and time-consuming. The advantages are that these wide band processes[12] involve the whole person in a relatively uncontrolled setting. They permit the decision maker to sample the candidate's behaviour over a wide area and obtain information which the formal test procedures cannot cover. Clinicians are not attempting specific predictions; they 'know' that each person is unique and hope to gain some understanding of his general attitude towards other people and what might be called his 'life-style'.

The statisticians and test constructors have a different purpose. They formulate hypotheses about people-in-general, isolating various characteristics, and then devise tests which follow a set pattern and are taken under controlled conditions in order to determine how one person compares with another. They are objective and relatively quick. A test of a certain skill can be used to predict performance in some activity requiring that skill. It is a betting game with the odds clearly stated. The odds on predicting cognitive skill—such as passing academic examinations—are higher (but nowhere near one hundred per cent) than the odds on—say—predicting skill in personal relationships.

Both approaches are valuable but the protagonists of each often behave like sworn enemies. George Miller in his valuable textbook 'Psychology—the Science of Mental Life'[13] has a very useful chapter on this topic,[14] which opens with this paragraph:—

'For several years there has been a running battle between the clinical heirs of Sigmund Freud and the statistical heirs of Sir Francis Galton. The Freudians learn about people by talking to them; the Galtonians give tests and compute statistics. When both groups are not both busy doing this, they like to spend their time criticising each other'.

In Britain at present the arch Galtonian is Eysenck who is optimistic about the future of objective measures and scornful of subjective ones. Philip Vernon, a man of at least equal stature scientifically, is highly sceptical.

'. . . we must insist . . . that empirically constructed tests and actuarial procedures show little prospect of providing the answer to all problems of personality assessment as many contemporary psychometrists would have us believe.'[15]

A good selection programme makes appropriate use of both approaches, and the definition of 'appropriate' varies with the circumstances. A situation—which can occur in a university department—where there are 200 suitably qualified applicants and only 30 places needs a different procedure from one in which all applicants could be accepted. In the latter case the selection procedure is concerned not with placing them in a ranking order but simply with determining their 'suitability'.

There are a number of objective tests and inventories (narrow band procedures) which can add useful information about would-be counsellors and caseworkers in addition to the ratings on interviews and group discussions. An intelligence test has already been mentioned: the non-verbal variety is probably fairer for adults of differing educational attainments: and this, together with either an attitude scale or a personality inventory, might be regarded as minimal.

A great deal of research has been done on attitude and personality testing and the interested reader must be referred to specific books on these subjects.[16] Attitude scales can be tailor-made to fit the problem but validation takes time and is essential. In order to illustrate the technique one such test will be described.

The Authoritarian (A) *Scale* devised by Adorno for a major American research[17] has some 'face validity' as a measure of prejudice and rigidity as against a more open 'democratic' attitude to people and their behaviour. Part of the study was concerned with anti-semitism and the test was first called the 'F' scale (F for fascist) but this highly emotive name is not now in general use.

The method of devising such scales is to decide the two extremes of the attitude it is required to measure (in this case Authoritarian/Democratic) and collect together a large number of statements which appear to discriminate between them. These are then given a pilot run with a reasonably large number of subjects i.e. large enough to give a breakdown of responses which is statistically respectable. Each statement is usually rated on a five point scale: agree strongly; agree; not certain; disagree; disagree strongly; and the ratings are then converted to numbers 1 to 5 or 5 to 1. This gives enough choice for the subject to do himself justice: a two-point 'forced choice' scale (Yes/No) is simpler but has disadvantages both for the subject and the tester.

Following a pilot run, a statistical device is used to compare scores on each item with the total score in order to detect which statements have not been scaled in the postulated direction i.e. which ones have proved ambiguous to the subjects. This is essential because the test is based on the assumption that adding together a score on each statement is meaningful. When the doubtful ones are eliminated the scale is ready for use. It should be emphasised that scales of this kind are 'self-rating' scales as are most personality tests. The subject tells the tester what his opinions are or how he thinks he would behave in certain circumstances *not* the other way round. Here are some statements taken from Adorno's scale:

'Obedience and respect for authority are the most important virtues children should learn.

'If people would talk less and work more, everybody would be better off.

'Young people sometimes get rebellious ideas, but as they grow up they ought to get over them and settle down.

'The business man and the manufacturer are more important to society than the artist and the professor.

'When a person has a problem or worry, it is best for him not to think about it, but to keep busy with more cheerful things.

'Nowadays more and more people are prying into matters that should remain personal and private.

'No weakness or difficulty can hold us back if we have enough will power.'

There are forty-four statements in all; others are concerned with attitudes to sex and sexual deviance; war and aggressiveness; power, religious belief and superstition.

Authoritarian attitudes score high on this scale: such a decision is quite arbitrary—they could equally well have been scored low but there must be an agreed direction for comparative purposes. However, Adorno made the mistake of constructing all his statements in the same direction (the ideal is half and half) so that strong agreement always earns a score of five and strong disagreement a score of one. The test is thus open to the criticism that it is partly a measure of acquiescence.[18] It is possible, but not yet conclusively demonstrated, that some people are more ready with a 'yes' response and that others tend towards answering 'no' regardless of the content of the question. Scores also correlate to some extent with the subject's degree of sophistication and show a small negative correlation with intelligence. However, the validity of scales of this kind does not rest on what the author *thinks* he is measuring but on whether the score predicts other types of behaviour satisfactorily. It is possible for the psychometrician to predict behaviour by means of tests without knowing why—i.e. without understanding the processes at work. This is where clinicians begin to feel that test results obscure the view. For the statistician the operative question is:— do the low scorers tend to make better counsellors than the high scorers? There is some indication that a test of this kind shows fair agreement with the subjective judgements of selectors and also experienced counsellors tend to have low scores but more research on this and similar tests would be valuable.

Paper and pencil tests can of course be open-ended and require the judge or selector to do the rating. These provide as it were a half-way house between the clinical and statistical approaches. A biographical essay is an obvious example, a variant of which requires the subjects to write two short self-descriptions one from the point of view of an admirer and the other purporting to be written by someone antagonistic. It is revealing to find how many people fail to carry out the instructions in the second case. They cannot be destructive about themselves and fall back on semi-complementary statements such as 'she is her own worst enemy'—'let's his heart run away with his head'—'tries to do too much' and so on.

How then should a counsellor selector programme be arranged to make the best use of the various techniques which have been mentioned, assuming that candidates have had an initial discussion to establish that they understand what is involved. There are three possible variants.

First there is the situation where the numbers accepted must be limited due to limited training facilities as is usually the case in the selection of social workers for full- or part-time courses in universities and colleges. The second case obtains when there are fewer candidates than there are places so that all those judged suitable can be accepted as tends to be the case, for example, with the National Marriage Guidance Council. The third variant which might more correctly be called placement rather than selection should be considered much more frequently than it is. Selection is usually thought of as a process in which the 'right' people are chosen to undergo a fixed treatment e.g. a course of training. The people must be suitable for the treatment. The question of varying the treatment to suit the people is rarely contemplated. It is of course administratively less tidy and would possibly in some cases increase the expense, but in the selection of older persons with varying backgrounds for counselling or social work it should be considered. There are circumstances in which it reduces the expense as, for example, when highly qualified candidates apply and are exempted from further selection and possibly also from some parts of the training.

Candidates for undergraduate places are usually fairly young and the emphasis tends to be on academic attainment with interviews to establish some measure of their motivation. Long training and close supervision on practical placements are relied upon to produce the necessary skills in human relationships and although there is some rejection it does not appear to be unduly high. Research in this area is badly needed. We do not know what type of individual fails to make the grade nor do we have any measure of the interpersonal competence of the 'qualified' social worker. Casual impressions suggest that not all of them would match up to stringent tests and assessment, but clearly development is satisfactory in most cases. One wonders whether there are wide personality differences on entry or whether they are all self-selected on the appropriate variables. Such questions need answering if we are to improve the training.

The more highly qualified social workers have of course taken postgraduate diploma courses of various kinds and here entrance is restricted and the candidate more carefully selected on personality grounds. This would apply also to those taking courses with the Institute of Marital Studies.

Mature students of moderate academic attainment who apply for college courses in social work need careful selection. The desire to 'work with people', so frequently expressed nowadays, is not enough. As with full-time students there is usually a restriction on entry so that candidates have to be placed in an order of merit and some 'suitable' candidates may have to be rejected. Otherwise the procedures should be the same as those for voluntary workers.

What should these be? How do we achieve the 'greatest yield of important relevant and interpretable information'? The following summary is based on the theoretical considerations outlined in this chapter.

1. Preferably a two-stage process with a minimum of two objective tests taken first. Some terminal decisions may with advantage be taken at this point. Two cut-off points on each test can be decided by experience so that the candidates are divided into three groups (good, doubtful, poor) the poor scorers being rejected. This means the lowest scorers on the intelligence test and for the Adorno Scale it would be the highest scorers, i.e. those with the most pronounced 'Authoritarian' attitudes. The 'good' and 'doubtful' groups might be named tentatively 'probably in' and 'probably out' but such a designation must be seen to be reversible.

Even if the selection procedure is completed in one stage there is still some advantage in designating the three groups by test results. To reverse the decision for the lowest scorers would need more potent evidence (including perhaps re-testing) than for the middle group.

2. Interviews. These can be programmed to dovetail with the discussion groups.

3. Two kinds of discussion group, one work centred and led by a selector and the other leaderless. Both need a selector to act as recorder.

The decision-making usually takes place after the candidates have dispersed and the selectors have had time to record all their ratings.

The test scores and the ratings cannot be used in any hard and fast way—their contribution to the final decision will differ from one candidate to another. For example, the decision to reject the lowest scoring group on the test results only, is a question of pay-off. The cut-off point is decided from experience as the point below which the chance of doing well is low and the cost of training in terms of time, money and personnel unjustified. Once this is decided it is uneconomic for the organisation and an unnecessary strain for the candidate to take any further part in the procedures.

With the average scorers one is looking for high personal ratings to decide whether they are 'in' and with 'high' scores one needs to know whether the personal qualities are so poor as to make the good scores of no account—that is, one is deciding whether they are 'out'.

The selection process can be approached in two ways. The one aims to ensure absolute fairness to each individual: the other accepts that this is a pipe dream and aims to minimise the cost in terms of money and time and maximise the odds in favour of success among the body of people finally chosen. If we search for absolute fairness we will burden ourselves and the candidates with large batteries of tests and prolonged assessments and the additional pay-off will be negligible. If we think in terms of pay-off and decision-making we will be parsimonious in choosing procedures; we will use each one sequentially to add to or detract from the results of the previous one and, in coming to the terminal decision, will take a practical and realistic view of the risks involved. The permissible risks must be decided in the light of the length and quality of the training offered. Where the training is adaptable risks can be lessened by also making choices about the best treatment.

In this section we have discussed selection in relation to counsellors and social workers which is of course a special case. In other situations the sequence of processes would vary. For example, the suitable placement of personnel in different kinds of jobs might entail interviews (wide bands) first to establish interests and preferences followed by objective tests (narrow bands) to determine the level of entry.

TRAINING

In the personal service professions training tends to be an on-going process with two interlinked and overlapping sections. There are first of all certain basic requirements for the job in terms of knowledge of facts and in terms of inter-personal behaviour. The theoretical bases of the interactions between client and counsellor have been discussed in Chapter 2 and what we need to consider here is the appropriate training methods to enable the counsellor to develop and understand them. Some of these have been mentioned already and need only to be listed. For the facts dealing with, for example, human growth and development and specific areas of social work, lectures, written notes and reading are required, followed by discussion. For the development of skills in interpersonal behaviour, some form of sensitivity training is essential.

At some point in the course of this basic training, practical work must begin: it is on the job that most of the learning about the job takes place. Supervision of the practical work is essential and will include case discussions with a group of colleagues and one to one tutorials centred on the individual student's own cases. The term 'case discussion' should be clearly distinguished from a 'case conference'. The latter brings together several professional workers who are working on the same case as, for example, a psychiatrist, psychologist and a psychiatric social worker in a child guidance clinic. In a case discussion each worker in turn may bring up one of his own cases and share his anxieties with his colleagues who in turn learn from his experiences. Such 'in-service' training can continue indefinitely since there is always something to be learned from a new client, but for economic reasons, if no other, it is likely to be less intense or less frequent as competence increases.

The aim of sensitivity training is twofold—sensitivity to others and the messages they convey and sensitivity about our own motives and behaviour. Learning about oneself in a group of this kind is difficult to describe but participants are never in doubt about the challenging nature of the experience. There are many texts, mostly American, analysing what goes on, generally in terms of group dynamics. Here are a few sub-headings from a table of contents of one of them.[19] Content versus feeling; Clarifying operations; The Show-How operations; Security-giving operations; The silent member; Talk as an avoidance technique; Cartharsis; The missing member; The missing leader; The monopolist.

Also stemming from the States are many attempts to find short cuts towards insightful learning, which, as carried out by means of group interaction, is unpredictable and often slow. Role playing is a useful technique in which each participant identifies with one of the characters in an invented situation such as a pay dispute—a lovers' quarrel—a family crisis—and improvises his part in it. Halfway through the period they can change roles and begin to identify with their erstwhile 'opponent'.

The process of listening and reflecting back can be isolated and practised as a separate exercise. Students pair off and engage in conversation: each item must be repeated back to the speaker to check its content and then again to interpret its feeling tone.

Experiments on the effect of eye contact can be tried. Student A by using his eyes must try hard to convey the impression that he is attending closely to what Student B is saying. A is the actor and B the detective. At first A will in fact listen to B carefully and sympathetically and then he will allow his mind but not his eyes to wander to an imaginary scene taking place behind B and then perhaps he will listen again but at the same time be thinking up a suitable answer. B must let A know whenever he feels that he is with him and when he senses that he is thinking of something else. A will discover how easily B detects the differences. We all note this kind of behaviour in other people but are generally unwilling to believe that when we ourselves act that way we can be 'seen through' just as easily. The main purpose of the exercises and indeed of the group discussion also is for students to be given information about the effects of their own behaviour on others.

'Exercises' devised more recently recognise the fact that feelings are communicated frequently, and for some people almost exclusively at the non-verbal and tactile level. In the States there is already more than one school of practice in this area and interested groups are growing in Great Britain. In some institutions for the mentally disturbed, experiments in treatment include physical encounters, both tender and coercive, between psychologists and patients. This approach in many ways runs counter to our culture: intellectual understanding is safe, tenderness and touching, except at the most intimate level, is in general, taboo. William Schultz, an American psychologist, provides an account of the theory and practice of these procedures in his book 'Joy: Expanding Human Awareness'.[20]

In social situations collusion to save each other from unpleasant truths is the general rule. In training for counselling we have to be made to face them. Some tutors practise shock tactics on the principle of learning to swim by being thrown in at the deep end. Others proceed more slowly and gently, hoping to make the process less painful. Either way some disturbance is inevitable.

Although the skills to be learned are similar, training schemes vary in practice. Also, in my experience, each particular professional group tends to develop its own style of behaviour, its own norms. Sensitivity training is certainly tackled in various ways. The T-group style in which feedback about our own behaviour comes from our peers within the group is very threatening and is rarely practised among young students in an academic setting. Reliance is placed on personal supervisors who can judge the rate of progress and offer the necessary level of support.

In the in-service training of groups of professional colleagues such as junior managers, teachers, youth workers, there are many hazards and it is essential for the leader to be highly competent, able and willing to expose himself to the threat of criticism. Indeed to attempt to train juniors by this method before the seniors have had experience of it is asking for trouble. If it is desired to change attitudes within an organisation the only feasible way is to start at the top—with the Principal, the Headmaster, the Youth Work Organiser or the Managing Director. Only then can the institution provide sufficient support and security to its members to make self-examination possible. To expose the junior members of a team only, imagining that they are the only ones who need to change their attitudes, is likely to produce pressures from below which will be seen as an attack. The assistant who finds himself out of sympathy with the ethos of his superior has three alternatives—fight, submission or flight—and flight to another job is the most likely outcome.

Voluntary bodies concerned with social work and counselling are perhaps at an advantage here. Certainly the style of in-service training offered by the National Marriage Guidance Council is more personal and more immediately challenging than is usually possible within a statutory body which, if we agree with Dr Woodhouse,[21] is fortunate since those particular counsellors are dealing with the intrinsically threatening subject of marital breakdown.

It is difficult to illustrate what is involved because a head-on challenge from one worker to another is a matter of the feelings generated, the shock of seeing ourselves as others are seeing us, and not a matter of the actual words spoken. Where the social work supervisor might proceed slowly and concentrate on the work being done hoping that her student would gradually begin to challenge herself, a small voluntary group can meet often enough to produce an atmosphere in which it is possible for members to be openly challenging of each other. The gaining of insight is accompanied by a sense of personal achievement but in the re-counting of it to others it usually sounds like a blinding glimpse of the obvious.

In a case discussion about a woman client who was very disturbed by her husband's indifference a counsellor's report dealt at length with her interviews with the husband whom she saw fairly regularly. She was cross-questioned: why did he come so often? what progress was he making? what was happening to the wife? The counsellor said he was very artistic and particularly fond of music and seemed to enjoy talking about it. 'And you seem to be enjoying it too', was the rejoinder which she was able, after some initial embarrassment, to accept.

A rather diffident and inadequate young man who had come to a counselling centre was reported (at a case discussion) to have said that his problem was 'girls'. 'I've never found a girl who would give me a second dance.' In the discussion which followed about how one could help young people who have such difficulties in their relationships with the opposite sex it transpired that the counsellor had not arranged to see him again. One colleague's immediate response was, 'So *you're* not giving him a second dance either!'

To see ourselves as others see us can be very painful. The

experiment is best tried in the safety of a closed group and residential training is the best means of achieving this quickly.

Laboratory or workshop training

Residential courses involving sensitivity training are frequently called 'laboratories' or 'workshops' and the participants may be referred to as 'delegates'. All such training groups are concerned with interpersonal competence and the emphasis may be on relationships at work or social relations in the community or on the more intimate and personal ones.

Delegates on laboratory training courses are usually housed in a comfortable hotel or conference centre, isolated from their day to day affairs, for a period of perhaps one to three weeks. They are expected to 'live in' on this 'cultural island' having only minimal contacts with job or family during the course. Such courses include a variety of activities and exercises but the T-groups into which the participants are divided (usually in groups of 10 to 15) are the major emotional focus of the whole experience. The aim of the T-group is to promote opportunities for learning and the beginner need waste no time since his own reactions to the novel experience are a proper starting point for study. We bring our own expectations to any new situation and, when these are not met, feelings of anger and aggression which are so often aroused towards organisers who seem to have let us down may well provide the first challenging topic for contemplation.

It is of course an essential prerequisite for success that the aims of a course are known to the participants, and they should not be assaulted by techniques for which they have given no permission. The difficulty with T-groups, however, is that members are in effect asked for a *carte blanche*. There is no set agenda: the group itself is the 'laboratory' in which human behaviour is generated and then observed. The element of risk is thus unavoidable and this places a considerable responsibility on the leader. He must walk a tightrope between allowing assumptions to be effectively challenged and insisting on adequate support for those members for whom the challenges are too threatening.

They are not always successful: indeed an adequate definition of a 'successful' group would be hard to come by. If genuine change takes place in the attitudes of a particular member, what does this do to his back home relationships either at work or within his family? Talking to a group of experienced teachers on a one year counselling training course I asked them what effect they felt it had had on themselves as persons and as teachers. A deputy headmistress replied 'I feel that my whole attitude to teaching and to the pupils has changed—I can't think what is going to happen when I get back to my school; I shall want to act quite differently and they won't know me'. Directors of firms ask 'Should we let old X go? What will it do to his marriage?'

It is equally hazardous if the changes are not genuine but merely superficial. Theorising about human relationships within departments might inspire a supervisor to air his newly acquired 'insights' and throw his weight about without making him any more competent in the promotion of changes of attitude among his colleagues.

In addition to the difficult question of 'what constitutes success?' there is also the problem of 'when does training finish?' The analysis of the counselling process as a semantic exercise[22] in which we, as counsellors are learning to translate the private languages of our clients suggests that when we stop learning we cease to be effective practitioners. In the personal service professions some form of continuing in-service support or consultation is at least desirable—some would say, essential—which raises the questions of the training of the trainers, variously known as tutors, supervisors or training officers. Clearly they must first be highly competent practitioners and they will need in addition the best external training courses that are available. Those run by the Tavistock Institute, the Grubb Institute, the National Marriage Guidance Council and various university departments are obvious examples.

The learning that takes place between a tutor and his student is mainly by example not by precept, so the counsellor who finds his tutorials supportive and not punitive will be the better able to accept his clients and appreciate their difficulties. The availability of this kind of tutorial support within the personal services varies very widely; the voluntary workers, often faring better than the statutory. The need for it is often misunderstood: there is the charge of being over-dependent and counsellors themselves sometimes ask 'when are we going to be allowed to stand on our own feet?'

There are several good answers. Since the work is open-ended and each case unique, workers need to be aware of the work done by their colleagues. They share a responsibility for the good name of their agency and they should share the anxieties. They provide a service for the community and must therefore know something about the community. They need to meet workers in other agencies and hear their views and in addition to being alert to changes in the outside world they need to keep an eye on changes within themselves. The confidences of clients must be kept but no agency can afford to allow its workers to be secretive. In other walks of life the quality of a person's performance is at least to some extent visible. In the personal services the client is the only observer and he is usually in no position to complain. Thus the obligation rests firmly with the performer to be constantly in search of ways in which he can improve the help he is offering.

As mentioned in Chapter 2,[23] some research results are now available on the efficacy of counselling and psychotherapy and the survey by Truax and Carkhuff is the most complete to date. Research in this area poses immense problems; practical, theoretical and statistical. In practical terms measures of personality variables for both participants—client and counsellor—are necessary; also a tape recording of each interview to allow several judges to listen and assess the extent of the rapport and finally some measures over a period, of personality or behavioural change on the part of the client. The theoretical questions relate to the choice of personality measures, the problem of the subjectivity of the judges' assessments and the elusive nature of the variables operating in a face to face encounter. Finally the problem of assessing the significance of changes of score over time on personality tests is by no means solved. Results can only be expressed in statistical terms. That is to say that changes of score in a positive direction on a personality test are more likely among clients of counsellors with personality variables A than with personality variables B. The operative phrase is 'more likely than'. There can be no certainty.

The counsellor personality variables most generally agreed by American research workers to be evidence of counsellor effectiveness are the 'therapeutic triad' suggested by Rogers in his book 'On Becoming a Person': accurate empathy, genuineness or congruence, and unconditional positive regard otherwise designated as non-possessive warmth. Truax and Carkhuff found that clients of counsellors rated high on these variables tended to have greater average positive changes of score on a personality test than clients of counsellors with lower ratings. To quote Allen and Whiteley[24] such a definition of success is 'not exceedingly compelling' because of course the averaging of results irons out the spread of individual scores and ratings. These authors go on to discuss the circumstances in which counselling as defined by Rogers and others is indicated and when 'behaviour modification' or operant conditioning as defined by the behaviourists is the method of choice. They cite for example the case of the unco-operative school child whose co-operative behaviour was greatly increased by teachers who 'were encouraged to shower her with unconditional positive regard'. The 'legitimate objectives' of counselling are not, they suggest, specific changes of behaviour which might more readily be brought about by other methods, but 'clarification of a person's internal frame of reference, the exposition of his basic assumptions about existence, his philosophy of life. There is the development of means to deal with the anxiety generated by guilt, meaninglessness, and the threat of death. There is the unravelling of the various conflicting forces that make the development of a viable sense of identity difficult'.[25]

Such considerations add another dimension to the difficulties of assessing the success of counselling. In addition to measures of personality and of personality change the expectation of clients and the aims of the counsellor need to be fairly precisely defined. Is it the client's behaviour or his environment that needs to be changed? How does the counsellor view the needs of his client? Is the aim specific or the general one of clarifying his self-concept and his attitude to life. It is likely that the relevance of the various criteria will vary within these varying counselling climates.

This is not a counsel of despair. A counsellor clearly should be aware of research results and sensitive to the various aspects of the counselling situation but the complexities are a reminder that he is practising an art and his success will vary according to his own strengths and weaknesses.

REFERENCES

1. See p. 41.
2. Cronbach and Gleser, *Psychological Tests and Personnel Decisions*, University of Illinois Press, 1957.
3. Cf. page 84, reference 28.
4. Vernon, P. E. and Parry, J. B., *Personnel selection in the British Forces*, Univ. of London Press, 1949. See also: B. S. Morris, *Officer Selection in the British Army*, 1942–45, *Occupational Psychology*, N.I.I.P., 1949, Vol. 23, pp. 219–34, where he discusses the validity and reliability of the procedures. This paper and related ones are reprinted in *Personality Assessment*, ed. by Boris Semeonoff, Penguin Modern Psychology Readings, 1966.
5. Wiseman, S., '*The marking of English Composition in Grammar School Selection*', British Journal Educational Psychology, 1949.
6. William H. Whyte Jnr., *The Organization Man*, Jonathan Cape, 1957, Appendix pp. 405–10, *How to Cheat on Personality Tests*.
7. In *Social Science and Social Pathology*, Allen & Unwin, Ch. IX, *Contemporary Attitudes in Social Work*, pp. 268–97. Also Appendix 2, *Professionalism in Social Work*, pp. 354–76.
8. See p. 84.
9. *The Use of Small Groups in Training*, Gosling, R., Miller, D. H., Turquet, P. M. and Woodhouse, D. L., The Tavistock Institute of Medical Psychology, 1967.

10. *The Marital Relationship as a Focus for Casework*, Report of Conference on the Implementations of Marital Interaction for the Social Services, Family Discussion Bureau, Codicote Press, 1962.

11. Gosling, Miller, Turquet and Woodhouse, *Ibid*, pp. 81–2.

12. P. 96, Reference 2.

13. Penguin Books, 1966.

14. *Ibid*, Ch. 20, *Clinical or Statistical*, pp. 337–50.

15. *Op cit.*, p. 422 (see Reference 16 below).

16. Boris Semeonoff's book is a good starting point (Reference 4 above). The following three papers are particularly relevant here:

    Eysenck, H. J. and Rachman, S., *Dimensions of Personality*, pp. 345–57.

    Edwards, A. L., *Social Desirability and Personality Test Construction*, pp. 387–403.

    Vernon, P. E., *The Concept of Validity in Personality Study*, pp. 407–23.

    This last is an abridged version of Ch. 13 of Vernon's book on *Personality Assessment*, Methuen, 1963.

    A standard work on attitude scales is Edwards, A. L., *Techniques of Attitude Scale Construction*, Appleton-Century-Crofts, 1957.

17. Adorno, T. W., Frenkel-Brunswik, Else, Levinson, D. J. and Sanford, R. N., *The Authoritarian Personality*, N.Y., Harper Bros., 1950.

18. See Conch, A. and Kemston, K., '*Yeasayers and Naysayers*' Agreeing response-set as a personality variable, Journal Abnormal Soc. Psychol., 60, 151–74, 1960.

19. Lipton, Walter M., *Working with Groups: Group Process and Individual Growth*, Wiley, N.Y., 2nd edition, 1966.

20. Grove Press Inc., N.Y., 1967 (Paperback 1969).

21. See p. 107.

22. See pp. 58–60.

23. Reference 19, p. 26.

24. Allen, Thomas W. and Whiteley, John M., *Dimensions of Effective Counselling*, Charles E. Merrill Publishing Co., Columbus, Ohio, 1968, p. 119.

25. *Ibid*, p. 122

Chapter 5

Practical Considerations

The foregoing theoretically based chapters must raise in the reader's mind many questions of a practical nature. Let us begin with the basic question 'who needs counsel'? We are all familiar with the gibe that very soon half the human race will be on the couch and the other half analysing them. As a Scottish psychiatrist of my acquaintance said 'the trrouble is—the categorries overrlap'. This fear finds expression in another form—a variant of Parkinson's Law; that the greater the provision of services the more people will seek help. The notion is that problems will be invented in sufficient numbers to keep the available therapists/counsellors fully occupied. What are the realities here? There are in this country approximately 3,368 child care officers and 3,351 full-time probation officers and the total number of children under 16 is 12,156,000. The local councils of the National Marriage Guidance Council had 19,366 new clients in 1969 and in the same year there were 50,063 divorces. All that can logically be said so far is that as provision of services increases they become better known to those who need them.

Counselling is a first-aid and preventive measure for people with a pain—a mental or emotional pain. If the pain is severe and serious it needs to be taken to the psychiatrist. The person who has no pain does not waste his time visiting a first-aid station or consulting a doctor. If, indeed, a person does go to the length of inventing a problem in order to talk to someone about it then clearly he has a problem.

Probably the only people in danger of inventing or searching for problems are adults who are longing to help the young and it is here that we need to ask the question 'who counsels who?' Examined closely 'The Adolescent Problem' may turn out to be

'The Middle-Age Problem'. Because the young create headaches for us we must not assume that it is they who need the aspirin.

What is the precise role of the counsellor and where does he fit into the social scene? Must it be a separately assigned role or can it be combined with others? Can a youth worker take time off from organising activities and managing his centre to counsel individual members? What are the problems of being a teacher one minute and a counsellor the next?

At present the idea of counselling is the 'in' thing—it is fashionable. It is often seen as *the* way of helping people and anything that smacks of advice or organising activities or teaching a few facts is seen as menial by comparison. There is a genuine dilemma. We know that learning is impaired by emotional disturbances; that the most important aspect of any encounter with the young is the interpersonal relationship; so it is perhaps understandable that teachers, youth workers, clergymen, community workers, probation officers and many others are tending to feel that solving emotional problems is more important work than any of their other jobs. At its worst this leads to people looking for problems and expecting to find them and the percipient young are not slow to sense this. From not taking the problems of adolescence seriously enough we are now sometimes in danger of being too solemn about them. More wit and humour and fewer agonies might help.

Counselling people whom one knows well socially is—to say the least—tricky and this goes for marriage guidance counsellors seeing their neighbours (which they never consent to do) and for youth workers seeing their own members or teachers their pupils. As I hope has been made clear in Chapters 2 and 4 one does not know and cannot foresee what will emerge in the course of a counselling or case work session. Anything of a deeply personal nature—sex, money, jobs, crime—is likely to be inhibited when talking to someone who is seen every day at work or over the garden wall. The need for privacy is felt particularly by adults. With young people it is not always so urgent. In many cases they are likely to prefer at first to talk to someone they already know and trust rather than go to a stranger. With transitory problems or sudden crises or difficulties amenable to discussion with peers it is clearly desirable to be able to consult the people on the spot. However, for young people to be in a position to seek help outside their own immediate circle may assist them in their search for identity and symbolise their emancipation. Befriending is an essential part of the job of teachers and youth workers and anyone responsible for young people, but counselling as defined in this book is a different job of work which cannot be done satisfactorily in the canteen over a quick cup of tea. It is a consultation to be undertaken deliberately requiring privacy and concentration. What the youth worker or teacher has to decide is how far the rest of his club or class will be able to cope if he devotes the necessary time to one member; whether it is of benefit to this member to talk to his youth leader rather than to a stranger whom he need never see again; whether his own training is adequate to deal with serious disturbances; whether the necessary professional support is available to him so that he can share his anxieties and examine his own involvement in the case and so on. In many instances the answer to all these questions has to be 'no'. These are some of the arguments for the provision of a central counselling service for young people manned by competent people whose training is an on-going process.

We need to make a distinction between the attitudes to people and their problems which underlie the counselling process and the process itself. Ideally all those engaged in the personal service professions need to share this attitude of accepting people as they are and to have an understanding of the notion of ambivalence and unconscious motivation: there should be a common core to their training so that they speak a common language. This does not imply—far from it—that everyone should function as a counsellor or—perish the thought—that in our day to day encounters with young people we should handle them as if they were clients. If I am angry and my colleagues treat me to a Rogerian Hm Hm I become murderous: if I do not see myself as a patient I am unlikely to accept therapy. The daughter of a friend returned from school one Friday evening tired and fed up. She flung her legs over the side of her chair and announced through gritted teeth that she was 'being an adolescent' and that she 'didn't want to be understood'. 'That's just as well', said her mother, 'because it's very difficult' and left her in peace. The counselling relationship though very personal is of a special kind in which the counsellor monitors his own behaviour for a particular purpose. It is not in any sense superior to the youth worker/member relationship or the teacher/pupil or the parent/child and it certainly lacks the vitality of the give and take of every day living. It is not 'everyday living'. Counsellors see their own ideas and beliefs as irrelevant in the counselling room but a youth worker or teacher without his own viewpoint or his own moral code or hierarchy of values would be disastrous. Normal young people, riding the ups and downs and the minor difficulties, want flesh and blood adults wearing their own clothes to argue with and disagree with, not someone permanently draped in the counsellor's raiment.

Many people find the idea of 'training' to be a counsellor puzzling if not downright silly. 'If you can get on with people it's just commonsense, isn't it?' 'People on buses are always telling me their problems—I must have sympathetic eyes'. The two encounters, in the bus and in the counselling room are quite different: the relationships are different and the objective is different. In the social situation we listen, sympathise and either reinforce the complainant in his own hunches or contradict and advise in the 'if I were you' manner. That is all that a social situation will stand, and to have a listener who is also friendly is very valuable. We all need a certain amount of warm affiliation with our fellow men and if one is willing to extend the use of the word, such friendly encounters are 'therapeutic.' They make us feel better.

This is not the role of the counsellor and training is essential in order to appreciate this. The beginner has to see and feel for himself—that 'pointing out', 'suggesting' and 'reasoning' with a person who has a genuine dilemma is no help to him at all: his problem has remained unsolved just because it is *not* amenable to such tactics. His prime need is for someone to accept that there is a problem, that there is no ready-made solution, and that the appropriate answer can only be found if he works for it. The student in training has to switch from the methods appropriate for dealing with factual situations where there is a 'right' answer to those which take account of feelings where the answer has to evolve from within the person. This paragraph can be repeated parrot-fashion by anyone: feeling the truth of it as a result of experience and acting on it is another matter.

This idea of a client 'working' to find a solution raises the question of *where* such work might be done. The assumption that counselling is best done in a separate consulting room and *not* as part of a domiciliary visit is often questioned: 'If you are dealing with family and relationship problems how can you possibly understand what is going on if you don't visit the people in their own homes?' Such a question raises several subsidiary questions. What, for example, is it that the counsellor is trying to 'understand'? If a person is in trouble within his family how possible is it for him to sit back calmly in his own home to consider the issues? If his main concern with the counsellor is to discover what he needs to do in his present circumstances—what in fact his task is—should this not be attempted out of range of all the other pressures that beset him?

Practical considerations such as housing and money clearly interact with emotional ones and in seeking help people in trouble strike a balance between them in selecting which particular agency to approach. What makes one husband visit the probation officer and another his local Marriage Guidance Council? One family might send for the police and another the mental welfare officer. It is plausible to assume that observable and measurable differences could be found between people who would tend to do the one and those who would be likely to do the other but there has been very little investigation of this so far. The person who chooses to knock on a door labelled 'Counselling' rather than one labelled 'Housing' has decided (possibly consciously but probably unconsciously) that if the quarrelling and hatred in their house could be dealt with they would be able to solve their accommodation difficulties. Similarly in the case of a student who is depressed a good teacher who helped him with his learning difficulties might prove to be the best first-aid but alternatively, counselling related—say—to his family relationships or his worry about his girl-friend might make it possible for him to get on with his studies without special help from his tutor. These are certainly among the assumptions implicit in the work of a counsellor. He does not see himself as called upon to go into the homes of his clients and sort out the numerous domestic problems of the families in difficulty (even if they wished him to do so) but he has learned from experience that if they are helped with their anxieties and their unhappiness the energy released will often be more than adequate to enable them to cope with the day-to-day practicalities themselves.

Of course this is a generalisation, a working assumption which may not be verified in practice. Then is the time to call for help from social work colleagues experienced in home visiting just as counsellors hope that social workers will recognise the need to consult a counsellor when it arises. Such co-operation and mutual help is essential if all the various needs are to be met. I have not mentioned in this context the stalwart work done by caseworkers in the Family Service Units simply because they are dealing with families so over-burdened with practical problems which they are unable to surmount that these must be tackled first before there is any hope of dealing directly with the relationship difficulties.

If, as I am suggesting, the 'Counsellor' restricts himself to a specific function then he will need to be able to call upon many other specialists to help in specific cases. Such dependence should be mutual: doctors, teachers, solicitors, social workers cannot always give up an hour a week for four or five weeks to listen while a particular patient, student or client talks. They must act, and advise and get to the end of the queue but somewhere in the system there must be someone whose job it is to listen.

However, even the Counsellor's time is not endless and just as it is generally necessary to confine each interview within a definite time span so must the relationship itself be brought to an end eventually. This happens ideally when the client has gained enough control over his situation to have no need of the

Counsellor's services, but not everyone is able to grow in this way and the counsellor must be alert to the danger of the client who ceases to work at his problem and shows signs of settling down into a dependent relationship.

In some way such a person must be made aware of the functional nature of the relationship—that it exists to promote movement and change and that increasing the independence of the client is the goal. If this is not being achieved the failure must be faced honestly and the implications discussed. If things can't be changed we have to learn to live with them. If this message is rejected at the verbal level it must be transmitted in action. A weaning process can begin by a progressive widening of the gap between meetings; starting with 'I'm afraid I'm unable to fit in a meeting with you next week' to a monthly interval and finally to 'Why not call me when you feel the need'. It is not uncommon for such imposed independence to produce signs of genuine self help. 'I missed coming but it wasn't as bad as I thought it might be.' Spectacular changes of attitude are rare and in many cases we have to be content if all that is achieved is less fantasy and a greater honesty in the recognition of failure.

Far from restricting the word 'counsel' in the way I am suggesting, the tendency at present is to widen it and if no attempt is made to bring order out of the creeping chaos the word will soon be simply a synonym for 'help'.

A form of treatment which relies on Behaviourist theory (as do the Behaviour Therapists) is sometimes referred to in American textbooks as 'Directive Counselling' in contradistinction to the term 'non-directive'. A young person complaining of an inability to make friends (or simply seen by his teacher to be having difficulties of this kind) might be 'directed' to go to a dancing class or to a youth club as a means of reducing his anxiety. This implies a considerable degree of control over the client's movements such as might be possible in an institutional setting and is indeed not far removed from teaching a youth to dance in order to increase his social skills. It is the reverse of the process we have been describing in which an attempt would be made to reduce the anxiety first in order to liberate the person to decide for himself whether it is a dancing-class or perhaps a sailing club that he would like to join.

As we saw in Chapter 2 'client-centred' or 'non-directive' procedures in no way violate behaviourist or learning theory so any claim that the so-called 'directive' method is more theoretically respectable is misleading. Whether to deal with the emotional or the practical issues first is a matter of choice in any particular situation and the 'directive' method may well be the method of choice in some circumstances but to call it counselling rather than treatment or training seems to me to cloud the issue. In child rearing, school teaching and youth club work we are constantly involved in cajoling the young to overcome their fear of the unknown by 'trying it out' while we actually or metaphorically hold their hands (i.e. reduce their anxiety). In some circumstances one might even 'direct' them to do so. Parents often do this. They try to predetermine the careers of their children by insisting on their undergoing rigorous instruction in musical performance, skating, athletics and other practical pursuits. Direction towards academic or any other mental work is not so easy but strong persuasion is common enough.

The use of the term 'vocational counselling' instead of 'vocational guidance' is another case in point. Clearly, all human activity has an emotional component but most people manage to take care of this themselves. Vocational guidance as generally understood is an attempt to increase the rationality of job choice. Objective measures of ability, aptitude and vocational preferences are obtained in order to give an individual sound advice about the various kinds of work likely to prove most suitable for him. This is not to say that decision-making about how to earn a living is not a highly charged affair but only a few will need 'counsel' about emotional difficulties. In a situation as universal as this the vast majority take it in their stride—it would be absurd to assume otherwise. There are difficult cases where perhaps ambition outruns ability or family tradition is affronted or fantasies about the dream job do not match the realities. Then it is the person or his family who needs help—the particular vocational choice involved is largely irrelevant. Obviously vocational guidance officers can be trained in counselling but this is not their primary task and if they are to counsel effectively when it is needed it should be clearly seen as separate and different from the diagnostic testing and the guidance issue. To build the counselling function into the title implies an expectation that it will be required in the majority of cases which is totally unrealistic and also unwise. We should always assume that the adolescent is capable of managing his own affairs until it is clear that he is not.

Having dealt with the word 'counsellor' in some detail we should perhaps turn our attention to the term 'client'. Many people find it ugly and unacceptable but none of the critics seem able to suggest an appropriate substitute. It means of course a person seeking professional services—a customer of a particular kind and if we accept that the customer is always right there is something to be said for its use in this context; the teacher, for example, should recognise when his pupil ceases to be *in statu pupillari* and becomes a 'customer'. In recognising the particular role of the counsellor in the social service this implies a particular role for the person in need of this kind of help. Those who feel it is a cold and impersonal word should remember than an element of detachment is an essential part of the relationship. Clients recognise this and welcome it. A woman who came to a 'walk in' service said to me 'I set off this morning to go to my sister's because I must talk to somebody about the trouble I'm in. But on the bus I thought "If I could get this thing sorted out she need never know" so I jumped off and came here'.

Also implied in this remark is the confidentiality of the counselling room which is another intrinsic aspect of such work. If we ask people to discuss their anxieties and declare their own weaknesses the need for complete privacy needs no argument. No information should ever be passed on to others without the person's consent. For this reason it is often argued that counselling services—for students, for example—should be clearly seen to be separate from 'authority' structures. Students must be confident that their troubles will not reach the ears of those who are going to assess their performance or write their testimonials.

One should of course avoid undue solemnity about this—by no means all that goes on in counselling needs to be marked 'highly secret' and by no means all clients—including students—are worried about confidentiality. Clients will often themselves disclose to others what has taken place and no counsellor should be naïve enough to accept at face value the statement that 'I have never told this to anyone else'. The point to be clear about is that the client is the arbiter; he controls what can be disclosed, not the counsellor. Any attempt to fit a counselling service into a wider framework either of the social services or of student provision must be made on this basis. I refer to the details of what is communicated and do not mean to imply that there can be no co-operation or case discussion of a general nature between casework colleagues bound by the same professional code on confidentiality. This may be necessary either for training purposes or to avoid overlap and duplication of effort.

As described in this book, counselling is a way of dealing with emotional and relationship distress by concentrating at least as much on the person and his feelings as on his 'problem'. It is considered as a specific function and there is no suggestion whatever that it is the only way of helping people: quite the reverse. People are helped in a great variety of ways by workers in the personal service professions and counselling is only one of them. It would be helpful if there were some general recognition of when counselling is appropriate and some general agreement about terminology.

As we move into the Seebohm era and attempt to co-ordinate the social services the roles of the various workers in the personal service professions should be more clearly defined and the skills required for the satisfactory performance of each role more clearly understood. This is not a plea for rigidity and demarcation lines. Many workers already play and will continue to play multiple roles but if they are to function effectively those responsible for training must know what skills are needed in each case and the workers themselves must be much more clearly aware of which function they are fulfilling, when.

There is a great deal of confusion at present. Teachers and

youth workers seldom meet and each group has only the haziest view of the role of the other. Clergy, probation officers and psychiatrists tend to work in isolation and rarely, if ever, discuss together their differing points of view on, for example, the individual's responsibility for his actions. The cleavage between the law and psychiatry here is a key dilemma of our time and has not yet been squarely faced. The suspicions and fantasies harboured against each other by professional caseworkers and voluntary counsellors remain submerged though neither group has any difficulty in recognising such unconscious conflicts among their clients.

This book is an attempt to clarify the job of the counsellor, a role which all of these workers may be called upon to play at some time. To restrict the use of the word 'counselling' to the kind of 'talking cure' which I have described, not only makes etymological sense but might clear away some of the fog. There is no area of social work in which woolliness and sentimentality are more beguiling and clarity of thought more elusive.

Bibliography

(Page numbers printed in bold at the end of an entry denote references in the text of this book.)

*ABERCROMBIE, M. L. JOHNSON. *The Anatomy of Judgement*, Penguin Books, 1969. 25p (4p). **81.**

— *Aims and Techniques of Group Teaching*, (in the press. Monograph of The Society for Research into Higher Education). **81.**

ADORNO, T. W., FRENKEL-BRUNSWIK, ELSE, LEVINSON, D. J. and SANFORD, R. N. *The Authoritarian Personality*, N.Y., Harper Bros., 1950. **111.**

ALLEN, THOMAS W. and WHITELEY, JOHN M. *Dimensions of Effective Counselling*, Charles E. Merrill Publishing Co., Columbus, Ohio, 1968. **124.**

ARBUCKLE, D. S. '*Five Philosophical Issues in Counselling*', Journal of Counselling Psychology, 1958. Reprinted in *Counselling Readings in Theory and Practice*, McGowan and Schmidt (eds.), Holt Rinehart & Winstone Inc., 1962. **23.**

*ARGYLE, MICHAEL. *The Psychology of Interpersonal Behaviour*, Penguin Books, 1967. 25p (4p). **41, 51, 54, 81.**

— *Social Interaction*, Methuen, 1969. £3·75 (10p). **54.**

BEECH, H. R. *Changing Man's Behaviour*, Penguin Books, 1969. 40p (5p). **40.**

BERNE, ERIC. *Games People Play. The Psychology of Human Relationships.* First published 1966. Penguin Books, 1970. 25p (4p). **50.**

BION, W. R. *The Leaderless Group Project*, Bull. Menninger Clinic 10, 1946. **84.**

BION, W. R. and RICKMAN, J. '*Intra-Group Tensions in Therapy*', Lancet, November 27th 1943. Reprinted in *Experiences in Groups and other papers*, W. R. Bion, Tavistock, 1961. (Social Science Paperback, 1968). 75p (7½p). **65.**

BRITISH INSTITUTE OF MANAGEMENT. Report on European Productivity Agency Project No. 399 on Group Dynamics, 1956. **83.**

*BROWN, J. A. C. *Freud and the Post-Freudians*, Penguin Books, 1961. 25p (4p). **18, 80.**

CHOMSKY. See LYONS, JOHN. **46.**

CONCH, A. and KEMSTON, K. '*Yeasayers and Naysayers*', Journal Abnormal Soc. Psychol. 60, 1960. **112.**

CRONBACH and GLESER. *Psychological Tests and Personnel Decisions*, University of Illinois Press, 1957. **96.**

EDWARDS, A. L. *Social Desirability and Personality Test Construction.* Reprinted in *Personality Assessment*, B. Semeonoff (ed.), q.v. **111.**

— *Techniques of Attitude Scale Construction*, Appleton-Century-Crofts, 1957. **111.**

EYSENCK, H. J. and RACHMAN, S. *Dimensions of Personality*. Reprinted in *Personality Assessment*, B. Semeonoff (ed.), q.v. **111.**

FOULKES, S. H. *On Group Analysis*, International Journal Psychoanalysis, Vol. 27, 1946. **65.**

FOULKES, S. H. and ANTHONY, E. J. *Group Psychotherapy*, Penguin Books, 1965. 25p (4p). **77.**

FLUGEL, J. C. *Man, Morals and Society*, Duckworth, 1945. **79.**

FREUD, SIGMUND. *The Interpretation of Dreams*, authorised translation by A. A. Burell, Allen & Unwin. First published 1913. **18.**

— *The Psychopathology of Everyday Life*, translated by Alan Tyson, paperback edition, Ernest Benn, 1966. 90p (10p). **57.**

FROMM, ERIC. *The Fear of Freedom*, Routledge & Kegan Paul, 1942. 60p (10p). **17.**

GESELL, ARNOLD. *The First Five Years of Life*, Harper & Row, 1940. **15.**

*GOFFMAN, ERVING. *Asylums*, Penguin Books, 1968. 40p (5p). **9.**

—*Behaviour in Public Places*, The Free Press, N.Y., 1963. **50, 51.**

GORER, G. and RICKMAN, J. *The People of Great Russia: A Psychological Study*, Cresset Press, 1949. **47.**

GOSLING, R., MILLER, D. H., TURQUET, P. M. and WOODHOUSE, D. L. *The Use of Small Groups in Training.* The Tavistock Institute of Medical Psychology, 1967. £1 (5p). **107, 109.**

GRUMMON, DONALD L. '*Client-Centred Theory*', Chapter 2 in *Theories of Counselling*, B. Stefflre, (ed.), q.v. **26.**

*HALMOS, P. *The Faith of the Counsellors*, Constable, 1965. **5.**

— *The Personal Service Society*, Inaugural Address, Cardiff, University of Wales Press, 1966. **12.**

— *The Personal Service Society*, Constable, 1970. £1·75 (20p).

HOMANS, G. C. *The Human Group*, Routledge & Kegan Paul, London, 1950. £1·75 (15p). **82.**

HORNEY, KAREN. *New Ways in Psychoanalysis*, Norton & Co., N.Y., 1939. **23.**

HUXLEY, A. *The Doors of Perception* and *Heaven and Hell*, Penguin Books, 1959. **29.**

ISAACS, SUSAN. *Intellectual Growth in Young Children*, Routledge & Kegan Paul. £1·50 (10p). **78.**

JAQUES, E. *The Changing Culture of a Factory*, Tavistock, 1951. **81.**

*KLEIN, JOSEPHINE. *The Study of Groups*, Routledge Paperback, 1967. 50p (5p). **67, 68, 76.**

KLEIN, MELANIE. *The Psychoanalysis of Children*, Hogarth Press, 1932. **77.**

KNIGHT, MARGARET. *William James*, Penguin Books, 1950. **14.**

KÖHLER, W. *The Mentality of Apes*, translated by Ella Winter, N.Y., Harcourt, Brace, 1925. Reissued Penguin Books, 1957. **37, 38**

LEWIN, K. *Principles of Topological Psychology*, translated by F. Heider and G. M. Heider, McGraw-Hill, 1936. **69, 70.**

— '*Field Theory and Learning*', Chapter 4 in *The Psychology of Learning*, Nat. Soc. Stud. Educ., 41st yearbook, Part II. N.Y., McGraw-Hill, 1936. **69.**

LIPPITT, R. *Training in Community Relations*, N.Y., Harper Bros., 1949. **83.**

LIPTON, WALTER M. *Working with Groups: Group Process and Individual Growth*, Wiley, N.Y., 1966. **117.**

LYONS, JOHN. *Chomsky*, Fontana Modern Masters Paperback, 1970. 40p (10p). **46.**

MEAD, G. H., *Mind, Self and Society—from the Standpoint of a Social Behaviourist*, University of Chicago Press, 1934. **49.**

MEDAWAR, SIR PETER. *The Art of the Soluble*, Methuen, 1967. £1·25 (10p). **2.**

*MILLER, GEORGE. *Psychology—the Science of Mental Life*, Penguin Books, 1966. 40p (10p). **110.**

OESER, O. A. *Teacher, Pupil and Task*, Tavistock, 1955. 80p (5p). **81.**

OTTAWAY, A. K. C. *Learning through Group Experience*, Routledge & Kegan, Paul, 1965. £2 (10p). **81.**

RICHARDSON, ELIZABETH. *Group Study for Teachers*, Routledge Paperback, 1967. 45p (4p). **81.**

ROGERS, C. R. *Counselling and Psychotherapy*, Houghton Mifflin Co., 1942. £3·75 (15p). **23, 24.**
— *Client Centred Therapy*, 1951. £1·50 (15p). **25.**
— *On Becoming a Person*, 1961. £2·25 (15p). **25.**
— *The Actualizing Tendency in Relation to Motives and Consciousness*, Nebraska Symposium on Motivation. University of Nebraska Press, 1963. **25.**
RUSSELL, B. *History of Western Philosophy*, Allen & Unwin, 1946. **38.**
*RYCROFT, C. (ed.) *Psychoanalysis Observed*, Constable paperback, London, 1966. 25p (4p). **58, 59.**
SCHEIN, E. H. and BENNIS, W. G. *Personal and Organizational Change through Group Methods*, John Wiley & Sons, N.Y., 1965. **73.**
SCHULTZ, WILLIAM C. *Joy: Expanding Human Awareness*, Grove Press Inc. N.Y., 1967. **119.**
SEEBOHM, F. (Chairman). Report of the Committee on Local Authority and Allied Personal Social Services, HMSO, 1968. £1·55 (10p). **7.**
SEMEONOFF, B. (ed.) *Personality Assessment*, Penguin Modern Psychology Readings, 1966. 50p (7½p). **97, 111.**
SKINNER, B. F. *Science and Human Behaviour*, Macmillan, 1953. £2·10 (15p). **56.**
— *Walden Two*. **56.**
STEFFLRE, B. (ed.) *Theories of Counselling*, McGraw-Hill, 1965. **13.**
SZASZ, THOMAS S. *The Myth of Mental Illness: Foundation of a Theory of Personal Conduct*, Secker & Warburg, 1961. £1·75 (10p). **49.**
THORNDIKE, E. L. *Animal Intelligence*, N.Y., Macmillan, 1911. **28.**
— *The Psychology of Learning*, N.Y. Teachers' College, 1913. **28.**
TRUAX, C. B. *Elements of Psychotherapy*. Discussion Papers, Wisconsin Psychiatric Institute No. 38, University of Wisconsin, 1962. **26.**
TRUAX, C. B. and CARKHUFF, R. R. *Towards Effective Counselling and Psychotherapy*, Chicago, Aldine, 1967. **26.**
*VERNON, M. D. *The Psychology of Perception*, Penguin Books, 1962. **53, 69.**
VERNON, P. E. *Personality Assessment*, Methuen, 1963.
— '*The Concept of Validity in Personality Study*' in *Personality Assessment*, B. Semeonoff (ed.) q.v. **110, 111.**
VERNON, P. E. and PARRY, J. B. *Personnel Selection in the British Forces*, University of London Press, 1949. **97.**

WALLIS, J. H. *Someone to Turn To*, Routledge & Kegan Paul, 1961. **6.**

WATSON, J. B. *Psychology from the Standpoint of a Behaviourist*, Philadelphia, Lippincott, 1919. **28.**

*WHYTE, L. L. *The Unconscious before Freud*, Tavistock, 1962. £1·25 (5p). **19, 20.**

WHYTE, W. H., JNR. *The Organization Man*, Penguin Books, 1957. 30p (4p). **100.**

WILLIAMS, JAMES. *The Marital Relationship as a Focus for Casework*, Report of a Conference on the Implications of Marital Interaction for the Social Services. Codicote Press, 1962. 40p (5p). **107.**

WINNICOTT, D. W. *Collected Papers*, London, Tavistock, 1958. £2·50 (10p). **78.**

WISEMAN, S. '*The Marking of English Composition in Grammar School Selection*', British Journal Educational Psychology, 1949. **97.**

RECOMMENDED READING

Books marked with an asterisk together with the following:

1. BORGER, R. and SEABORNE, A. E. M. *The Psychology of Learning*, Penguin Books, 1966. 25p (4p)
2. FOSS, BRIAN M. (ed.) *New Horizons in Psychology*, Penguin Books, 1966, especially pp. 152–166 on Psycholinguistics. 40p (5p)
3. GOFFMAN, ERVING. *Stigma*, Penguin Books, 1968. 25p (4p)
4. LYTTON, HUGH. *School Counselling and Counsellor Education in the United States*, Nat. Foundation for Educational Research, 1968.

REFERENCES

Penguin Books publish several excellent series dealing with psychological topics. They are:—

Modern Psychology Readings which contain a selection of original papers on each particular subject;

The Science of Behaviour series and *Pelican Books on Psychology* edited by C. A. Mace.

Wherever feasible these or other paperbacks have been chosen for reference rather than more expensive hardbacks.

NOTE

Many of the books listed are shown with price and postage (in brackets). These are available from the NMGC Book Shop, 58 Queen Anne Street, London W1M 0BT.

Index